The soup bible

The soup bible

All the soups you could ever need in one inspiring collection

Consultant Editor
DEBRA MAYHEW

HERMES HOUSE

This edition is published by Hermes House

Hermes House is an imprint of Anness Publishing Ltd
Hermes House, 88–89 Blackfriars Road, London SE1 8HA
tel. 020 7401 2077; fax 020 7633 9499; info@anness.com

A CIP catalogue record for this book is available from the British Library

Publisher: Joanna Lorenz; *Editor:* Debra Mayhew;
Production Controller: Ann Childers; *Editorial Reader:* Hayley Kerr
Designer: Bill Mason; *Illustrator:* Anna Koska.

Recipe Contributors: Catherine Atkinson, Alex Barker, Michelle Berriedale-Johnson, Anglela Boggiano,
Janet Brinkworth, Carla Capalbo, Kit Chan, Jacqueline Clark, Maxine Clark, Frances Cleary,
Carole Clements, Andi Clevely, Trish Davies, Roz Denny, Patrizia Diemling, Matthew Drennan,
Sarah Edmonds, Joanna Farrow, Rafi Fernandez, Christine France, Sarah Gates, Shirley Gill,
Rosamund Grant, Rebekah Hassan, Deh-Ta Hsiung, Shehzad Husain, Judy Jackson, Sheila Kimberley,
Masaki Ko, Elisabeth Lambert Ortiz, Ruby Le Bois, Gilly Love, Lesley Mackley, Norma MacMillan,
Sue Maggs, Kathy Man, Sallie Morris, Annie Nichols, Maggie Pannell, Katherine Richmond, Anne
Sheasby, Jenny Stacey, Liz Trigg, Hilaire Walden, Laura Washburn, Steven Wheeler, Kate Whiteman,
Elizabeth Wolf-Cohen, Jeni Wright.

Photographers: Karl Adamson, Edward Allwright, David Armstrong, Steve Baxter, James Duncan,
John Freeman, Ian Garlick, Michelle Garrett, Amanda Heywood, Janine Hosegood, David Jordan,
William Lingwood, Patrick McLeary, Michael Michaels, Thomas Odulate, Juliet Piddington, Peter Reilly.

Also published as *Soup*

1 3 5 7 9 10 8 6 4 2

NOTES

Standard spoon and cup measures are level.

Large eggs are used unless otherwise stated.

CONTENTS

Introduction

YOU WILL FIND PLENTY in these pages to inspire you: Cold, light soups to refresh your palate on a hot summer's day; rich and creamy soups to slide like velvet over your taste buds; spicy soups to warm and comfort you on cold winter days; and hearty soups, full of goodness, to provide a satisfying lunch when hunger strikes. Here, in one collection, are soups for all occasions.

Few dishes give more all-round pleasure than a good homemade soup, so it is hardly surprising soups feature in every cuisine around the world—as users of this book will discover—whether they are called gumbos, potages, broths, chowders, or consommés. Now that once-unfamiliar ingredients are readily available in specialist ethnic grocery stores and many supermarkets, the world of soups is yours to explore.

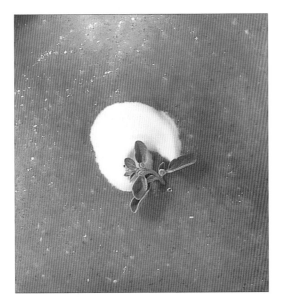

Visit continental Europe and sample diverse delights such as the filling pistou from France, cooling gazpacho from Spain, or warming Lentil and Bacon Soup from Germany. Try a traditional Smoked Haddock and Potato Soup from the British Isles or fruity soups from central Europe, like Romania's Apple Soup, or classic borscht from Russia. Be tempted by soups from the African continent such as Chicken Soup with

Vermicelli from Morocco, or Smoked Cod
and Okra Soup from Ghana. The East
beckons with piquant and translucent
soups, such as the traditional Hot-and-Sour
Soup from China and the stunning Shrimp
Ball and Egg Knot Soup from Japan. Make
sure you don't miss Louisiana's Sausage
and Seafood Gumbo, or Mexico's Jalapeño-
Style Soup with chicken, chili and avocado.

Good soup is easy to make, especially if you
use the freshest ingredients, when thy are in
season. A good stock is necessary as the basis for
many—though by no means all—soups. It takes
time to make, but large quantities can be
prepared in advance and frozen in smaller
portions to await a bout of soup making at your
convenience. Recipes for basic vegetable, fish,
meat, poultry, Chinese, and Japanese stocks are
given in the following pages.

The right garnish, too, enhances even
the simplest soup; giving careful thought
to the presentation of your soup adds a
professional finish. Herby croutons or
crunchy leek haystacks, for example,
arranged in the center of your soup add a
contrasting texture and a complementary
flavor. Try the suggested garnishes in this
book, then have fun developing your own
perfect finishes.

Each soup recipe in this collection features step-by-step directions, many illustrated, to guide you through the soup-making process. Beautiful color photographs show the finished dish. So take your time to try many of the delicious recipes featured here. You will soon grow in confidence and begin to change the basic recipes in this book, and create your own personalized favorites.

Anyone who does not eat meat or fish should look for the special symbol V beside recipes to indicate they are suitable for vegetarians. These recipes do not contain any meat or fish products, but may contain cheese; vegetarian varieties of cheese can be substituted if desired. A recipe for a vegetarian version of Japanese dashi is suggested alongside the traditional version. Also, in the vegetable or bean soups that include chicken stock, feel free to substitute vegetable stock.

If you have yet to experience the satisfaction gained from making and eating your own soup at home, or if you are an experienced soup maker and want to increase your repertoire of recipes, you need look no farther than the pages of this beautifully illustrated book for inspiration. Turn the page and savor the recipes.

Making stocks

Fresh stocks are indispensable for creating good homemade soups. They add a depth of flavor that plain water just cannot achieve.

Although many supermarkets sell tubs of fresh stock, these are expensive, especially if you need large quantities for your cooking. Making your own is surprisingly easy, and much more economical, particularly if you can use leftovers—the chicken carcass from Sunday lunch, for example, or the shells left from shelling shrimp. But homemade stocks aren't just cheaper, they're also a lot tastier and they can be much more nutritious, too, precisely because they're made with fresh, natural ingredients.

You can, of course, use bouillon cubes or granules, but be sure to check the seasoning as these are often very high in salt.

One good idea for keen and regular soup makers is to freeze homemade stock in plastic freezer bags, or ice-cube trays so you always have a supply at your disposal. Frozen stock can be stored in the freezer for up to six months. Make sure that you label each stock carefully for easy identification.

Use the appropriate stock for the soup you are making. Onion soup, for example, is improved with a good beef stock. Be particularly careful to use a vegetable stock if you are catering for vegetarians.

Recipes are given on the following pages for vegetable stock, chicken stock, meat stock, fish stock, and basic stocks for Chinese and Japanese cooking.

Vegetable Stock

V

Use this versatile stock as the basis for all vegetarian soups.

INGREDIENTS

Makes 2¾ quarts

2 leeks, roughly chopped

3 celery stalks, roughly chopped

1 large onion, with skin, chopped

2 pieces fresh ginger root, chopped

1 yellow bell pepper, seeded and chopped

1 parsnip, chopped

mushroom stalks

tomato peelings

3 tablespoons light soy sauce

3 bay leaves

a bunch of parsley stems

3 sprigs of fresh thyme

1 sprig of fresh rosemary

2 teaspoons salt

freshly ground black pepper

3¾ quarts cold water

1 Put all the ingredients into a very large saucepan. Bring slowly to a boil. Lower the heat and simmer for 30 minutes, stirring from time to time.

2 Leave to cool. Strain, then discard the vegetables: The stock is ready to use. Alternatively, chill or freeze the stock and keep it to use as required.

Fish Stock

Fish stock is much quicker to make than poultry or meat stock. Ask your fishmonger for heads, bones, and trimmings from white fish.

INGREDIENTS

Makes about 1 quart

1½ pounds heads, bones, and trimmings
   from white fish

1 onion, sliced

2 celery stalks with leaves, chopped

1 carrot, sliced

½ lemon, sliced (optional)

1 bay leaf

a few sprigs of fresh parsley

6 black peppercorns

1½ quarts cold water

⅔ cup dry white wine

1 Rinse the fish heads, bones, and trimmings well under cold water. Put in a stockpot with the vegetables and lemon, if using, the herbs, peppercorns, water, and wine. Bring to a boil, skimming the surface frequently. Lower the heat and simmer for 25 minutes.

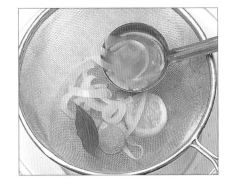

2 Strain the stock without pressing down on the ingredients in the strainer. If not using immediately, leave to cool and refrigerate. Fish stock should be used within 2 days, or it can be frozen for up to 3 months.

Chicken Stock

A good home-made poultry stock is invaluable in the kitchen. If poultry giblets are available, add them (except the livers) with the wings. Once made, chicken stock can be kept in an airtight container in the refrigerator for 3 to 4 days, or frozen for up to 6 months.

INGREDIENTS

Makes about 2¾ quarts

2½ to 3 pounds chicken or turkey
   (wings, backs, and necks)
2 onions, unpeeled, quartered
1 tablespoon olive oil
4¼ quarts cold water
2 carrots, roughly chopped
2 celery stalks, with leaves,
   roughly chopped
a small handful of fresh parsley
a few sprigs of fresh thyme, or
   ¾ teaspoon dried thyme
1 or 2 bay leaves
10 black peppercorns, lightly crushed

1 Combine the poultry wings, backs, and necks in a stockpot with the onion quarters and the oil. Cook over medium heat, stirring occasionally, until the poultry and onions are lightly and evenly brown.

2 Add the water and stir well to mix in the sediment on the bottom of the pan. Bring to a boil and skim off the impurities as they rise to the surface of the stock.

3 Add the chopped carrots and celery, fresh parsley, thyme, bay leaf, and black peppercorns. Lower the heat, partly cover the stockpot and simmer the stock for about 3 hours.

4 Strain the stock through a strainer into a bowl and leave to cool. Chill in the refrigerator for an hour.

5 When cold, carefully remove the layer of fat that will have set on the surface. Store in the refrigerator for 3 to 4 days, or freeze until required.

Meat Stock

The most delicious meat soups rely on a good homemade stock for success. A bouillon cube will do if you do not have time to make your own. Once it is made, meat stock can be kept in the refrigerator for up to 4 or 5 days, or you may freeze it for longer storage.

INGREDIENTS

Makes about 2¼ quarts

4 pounds beef bones, such as shin, leg, neck, and shank, or veal or lamb bones, cut into 2½-inch pieces

2 onions, unpeeled and quartered

2 carrots, roughly chopped

2 celery stalks, with leaves, roughly chopped

2 tomatoes, coarsely chopped

5 quarts cold water

a handful of parsley stems

few sprigs of fresh thyme or ¾ teaspoon dried thyme

2 bay leaves

10 black peppercorns, lightly crushed

1 Preheat the oven to 450°F. Put the bones in a roasting pan and roast, turning them occasionally, for 30 minutes until they start to brown.

2 Add the onions, carrots, celery, and tomatoes and baste with the fat in the pan. Roast for 20 to 30 minutes longer until the bones are very brown. Stir and baste occasionally.

3 Transfer the bones and roasted vegetables to a stockpot. Spoon off the fat from the roasting tin. Add a little of the water to the roasting pan and bring to a boil on the stovetop, stirring well to scrape up any brown bits. Pour this liquid into the stockpot.

4 Add the remaining water to the pot. Bring just to a boil, skimming frequently to remove all the foam from the surface. Add the parsley, thyme, bay leaves, and peppercorns.

5 Lower the heat, partly cover the pot, and simmer the stock for 4 to 6 hours. The bones and vegetables should always be covered with liquid, so top up with a little boiling water from time to time if necessary.

6 Strain the stock through a colander. Skim as much fat as possible from the surface. If possible, cool the stock and then refrigerate it: The fat will rise to the top and set in a layer that can be removed easily.

Stock for Chinese Cooking

This stock is an excellent basis for soup making.

INGREDIENTS

Makes 2¾ quarts

1½ pounds chicken portions

1½ pounds spareribs

4 quarts cold water

3 or 4 pieces fresh ginger root, unpeeled, crushed

3 or 4 scallions, each tied into a knot

3 to 4 tablespoons Chinese rice wine or dry sherry

1 Trim off any excess fat from the chicken and spareribs. Chop them into large pieces.

2 Place the chicken and sparerib pieces into a large stockpot with the water. Add the ginger and scallion knots.

3 Bring to a boil and, using a strainer, skim off the froth. Lower the heat and simmer, uncovered, for 2 to 3 hours.

4 Strain the stock, discarding the chicken, pork, ginger, and scallions. Add the wine or sherry and return to a boil. Lower the heat and simmer for 2 to 3 minutes. Refrigerate the stock when cool: It will keep for up to 4–5 days. Alternatively, it can be frozen in small containers for use when required.

Stock for Japanese Cooking

Dashi *is the stock that gives the characteristically Japanese flavor to many dishes. Known as Ichiban-dashi, it is used for delicately flavored dishes, including soups. Of course, instant stock is available in all Japanese supermarkets, either in granular form, in concentrate, or even in a tea bag. Follow the directions on the package.*

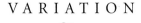

INGREDIENTS

Makes about 3½ cups

¼ ounce dried kombu seaweed

¼ to ½ oz bonito flakes

VARIATION

For vegetarian dashi, omit the bonito flakes (dried tuna) and follow the same method.

1 Wipe the kombu seaweed with a damp cloth and cut 2 slits in it with scissors, so it flavors the stock effectively.

2 Soak the kombu in 3¾ cups cold water for 30 to 60 minutes.

3 Heat the kombu in its soaking water over medium heat. Just before the water boils, remove the seaweed. Add the bonito flakes and bring to a boil over high heat. Remove the pan from the heat.

4 Leave the stock until all the bonito flakes sink to the bottom of the pan. Line a strainer with paper towels or cheesecloth and place it over a large mixing bowl. Slowly pour the stock through it.

V

Garnishes

Sometimes, a soup needs something to lift it out of the ordinary, and garnishes are the answer. They are an important finishing touch, adding a little extra to soups; they not only look good, but can add an extra dimension to the flavor. A garnish can be as simple as a sprinkling of chopped parsley, a swirl of cream, or some freshly grated cheese. Alternatively, it can be something that requires a little more attention, such as homemade croutons or sippets. All the garnishes featured here are suitable for vegetarians.

DUMPLINGS

These dumplings are easy to make and add an attractive and tasty finishing touch to country-style soups.

INGREDIENTS

½ cup semolina or all-purpose flour
1 egg, beaten
3 tablespoons milk or water
a generous pinch of salt
1 tablespoon chopped fresh parsley

1 Mix all the ingredients together to form a soft, elastic dough. Leave to stand, covered with plastic wrap, for 5 to 10 minutes.

2 Drop small rounded spoonfuls of the dough into the soup and cook for 10 minutes until firm.

CRISPY CROUTONS

Croutons add a delicious crunchy texture to creamy soups, and are a good way of using up stale bread. Use thinly sliced ciabatta or French bread for good results.

INGREDIENTS

bread
good-quality, flavorless oil, such as sunflower or peanut; or, for a fuller flavor, extra-virgin olive oil; or a flavored oil such as one with garlic and herbs or chili

1 Preheat the oven to 400°F. Cut the bread into small cubes and place on a cookie sheet, taking care that they do not overlap.

2 Brush with your chosen oil. Bake for about 15 minutes until golden and crisp. Leave to cool: They crisp up more as they cool.

3 Store the croutons in an airtight container for up to a week. Reheat in a warm oven, if liked, before serving.

RIVELS

Rivels are pea-size pieces of dough that swell when cooked in a soup.

INGREDIENTS

1 egg
¾ to 1 cup all-purpose flour
½ teaspoon salt
freshly ground black pepper

1 Beat the egg in a bowl. Add the flour, salt, and pepper to taste and stir with a wooden spoon. Finish mixing with your fingers, rubbing to blend the egg and flour together to form pea-size pieces.

2 Bring the soup back to the boil. Sprinkle in the pieces of dough, stirring gently.

3 Lower the heat and simmer for about 6 minutes until the rivels swell slightly and are cooked through. Serve at once.

SWIRLED CREAM

A swirl of cream is the classic finish for many soups, such as a smooth tomato soup or chilled asparagus soup. It gives a professional finish to your soup, although the technique is simplicity itself.

INGREDIENTS

light cream

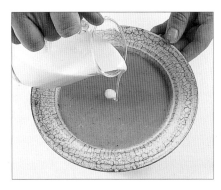

1 Transfer the cream into a pitcher with a good pouring lip. Pour a swirl onto the surface of each bowl of soup.

2 Draw the tip of a fine skewer quickly backward and forward through the cream to create a delicate pattern. Serve the soup immediately.

SIPPETS

Another good way of using up slightly stale bread, sippets are larger than croutons and have a more intense flavor because of the addition of fresh herbs. Experiment with the herbs according to the flavor of the soup.

INGREDIENTS

3 slices day-old bread
4 tablespoons butter
3 tablespoons finely chopped fresh
    parsley, or cilantro or basil

1 Cut the bread into fingers about 1 inch long.

2 Melt the butter into a large skillet. Toss in the small fingers of bread and fry slowly until golden brown.

3 Add the fresh herbs and stir well to combine. Cook for 1 minute longer, stirring continuously. Strew the sippets on top of the soup and serve.

LEEK HAYSTACKS

Stacks of golden leek look good served on a creamy soup and the crunchy texture contrasts well with the smoothness of the soup.

INGREDIENTS

1 large leek
2 tablespoons all-purpose flour
oil for deep frying

1 Slice the leek in half lengthwise and then cut into quarters. Cut into 2-inch and then into very fine strips. Place in a bowl, sprinkle the flour over, and toss to coat.

2 Heat the oil to 325°F. Drop small spoonfuls of the floured leeks into the oil and cook for 30 to 45 seconds until golden. Drain on paper towels. Repeat with the remaining leeks.

3 Serve the soup with a small stack of leeks piled on top of each bowl.

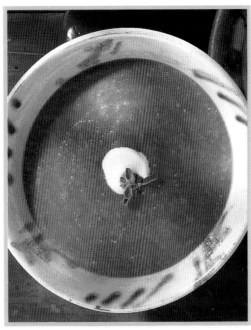

LIGHT &
REFRESHING
SOUPS

Chilled Asparagus Soup

This delicate, pale green soup, garnished with a swirl of cream or yogurt, is as pretty as it is delicious.

INGREDIENTS

Serves 6

2 pounds fresh asparagus

4 tablespoons butter or olive oil

1½ cups sliced leeks or scallions

3 tablespoons all-purpose flour

6¼ cups chicken stock or water

½ cup light cream or plain yogurt

1 tablespoon chopped fresh tarragon or chervil

salt and freshly ground black pepper

3 Heat the butter or oil in a heavy-bottomed saucepan. Add the sliced leeks or scallions and cook over low heat for 5 to 8 minutes until soft but not brown. Stir in the chopped asparagus stalks, cover, and cook for 6 to 8 minutes longer until the stalks are tender.

4 Add the flour and stir well to blend. Cook for 3 to 4 minutes, uncovered, stirring occasionally.

5 Add the stock or water. Bring to a boil, stirring frequently. Lower the heat and simmer for 30 minutes. Season with salt and pepper.

6 Purée the soup in a food processor or food mill. If necessary, strain it to remove any coarse fibers. Stir in the asparagus tips, most of the cream or yogurt, and the herbs. Chill well. Stir before serving and check the seasoning. Garnish each bowl with a swirl of cream or yogurt.

1 Cut the top 2½ inches off the asparagus spears and blanch the tips in boiling water for 5 to 6 minutes until just tender. Drain thoroughly. Cut each tip into 2 or 3 pieces, set aside.

2 Trim the ends of the stalks, removing any brown or woody parts. Chop the stalks into ½-inch pieces.

Miami Chilled Avocado Soup

Avocados are combined with lemon juice, dry sherry and an optional dash of hot-pepper sauce, to make this subtle chilled soup.

INGREDIENTS

Serves 4

2 large or 3 medium ripe avocados

1 tablespoon fresh lemon juice

¾ cup coarsely chopped peeled and
  seeded cucumber

2 tablespoons dry sherry

¼ cup coarsely chopped scallions, with
  some of the green stems

2 cups mild-flavored chicken stock

1 teaspoon salt

hot-pepper sauce (optional)

plain yogurt or light cream, to garnish

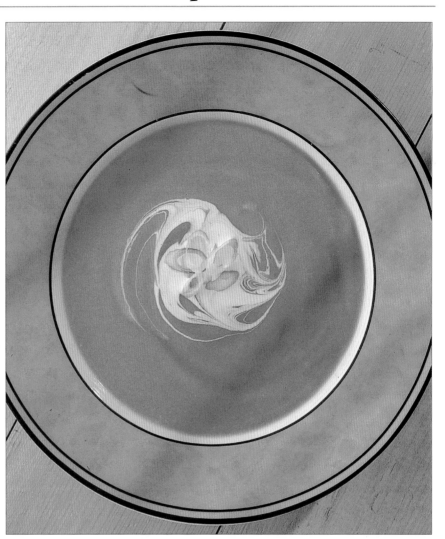

1 Cut the avocados in half, remove the pits, and peel. Coarsely chop the flesh and place in a food processor or blender. Add the lemon juice and process until very smooth.

2 Add the cucumber, sherry, and most of the scallions, reserving a few for the garnish. Process again until smooth.

3 In a large bowl, combine the avocado mixture with the chicken stock. Whisk until well blended. Season with the salt and a few drops of hot-pepper sauce, if liked. Cover the bowl and place in the refrigerator to chill thoroughly.

4 To serve, fill individual bowls with the soup. Place a spoonful of yogurt or cream in the center of each bowl and swirl with a spoon. Sprinkle with the reserved chopped scallions.

Vichyssoise

Serve this flavorful soup with a dollop of crème fraîche or sour cream and sprinkle with a few snipped fresh chives—or, for special occasions, garnish with a small spoonful of caviar or lumpfish caviar.

INGREDIENTS

Serves 6 to 8

about 3 large potatoes, peeled
   and cubed

1½ quarts chicken stock

12 ounces leeks, trimmed

⅔ cup crème fraîche or sour cream

salt and freshly ground black pepper

3 tablespoons snipped fresh chives,
   to garnish

1 Put the cubed potatoes and chicken stock in a saucepan or flameproof casserole and bring to a boil. Lower the heat and simmer for 15 to 20 minutes.

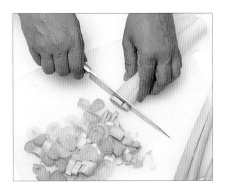

2 Make a slit along the length of each leek and rinse well under cold running water to wash away any dirt or grit. Slice thinly.

VARIATION

To make a low-fat soup, use fromage blanc made with skim milk instead of crème fraîche or sour cream.

3 When the potatoes are almost tender, stir in the leeks. Taste and season with salt and freshly ground black pepper. Simmer for 10 to 15 minutes until both vegetables are soft, stirring occasionally. If the soup is too thick, thin it down with a little more stock or water.

4 Purée in a blender or food processor: If you prefer a very smooth soup, process it in a food mill or press through a coarse strainer. Stir in most of the crème fraîche or sour cream. Cool and then chill. To serve, ladle into chilled bowls and garnish with a swirl of cream and the chives.

Gazpacho

This traditional, chilled Spanish soup is perfect for a summer lunch. Make sure all the ingredients are in peak condition for the best-flavored soup.

INGREDIENTS

Serves 6

1 green bell pepper, seeded and roughly chopped

1 red bell pepper, seeded and roughly chopped

½ cucumber, roughly chopped

1 onion, roughly chopped

1 fresh red chili, seeded and roughly chopped

3 cups roughly chopped ripe plum tomatoes

3¾ cups passata (strained puréed tomatoes) or tomato juice

2 tablespoons red-wine vinegar

2 tablespoons olive oil

1 tablespoon caster sugar

salt and freshly ground black pepper

crushed ice, to garnish (optional)

1 Reserve a small piece of the green and red bell peppers, the cucumber, and the onion. Finely chop these and set aside as a garnish.

2 Process all the remaining ingredients, except the ice, in a blender or food processor until smooth: You may need to do this in batches.

3 Press the soup through a strainer into a clean glass bowl, pushing it through with a spoon to extract the maximum amount of flavor.

4 Adjust the seasoning and chill. Serve sprinkled with the reserved chopped green and red bell peppers, cucumber, and onion. For a finishing touch, add a little crushed ice to the garnish.

V

Summer Tomato Soup

The success of this soup depends on having ripe, full-flavored tomatoes, such as an oval plum variety, so make this when the tomato season is at its peak.

INGREDIENTS

Serves 4

1 tablespoon olive oil

1 large onion, chopped

1 carrot, chopped

2¼ pounds ripe tomatoes, quartered

2 garlic cloves, chopped

5 sprigs of fresh thyme, or ¼ teaspoon
   dried thyme

4 or 5 sprigs of fresh marjoram, or
   ¼ teaspoon dried marjoram

1 bay leaf

3 tablespoons crème fraîche, sour cream,
   or plain yogurt, plus a little extra
   to garnish

salt and freshly ground black pepper

1 Heat the olive oil in a large,
preferably stainless-steel,
saucepan or flameproof casserole.

2 Add the onion and carrot and
cook over medium heat for
3 to 4 minutes until just soft,
stirring occasionally.

3 Add the quartered tomatoes,
chopped garlic, and herbs.
Lower the heat and simmer,
covered, for 30 minutes.

4 Discard the bay leaf. Strain the
soup. Stir in the cream or
yogurt and season. Leave to cool,
then chill in the refrigerator.

VARIATION
〜

If you prefer, use oregano instead
of marjoram, and parsley
instead of thyme.

Watercress and Orange Soup

V

This healthy and refreshing soup is just as good served either hot or chilled.

INGREDIENTS

Serves 4

1 large onion, chopped
1 tablespoon olive oil
2 bunches or bags of watercress
grated peel and juice of 1 large orange
2½ cups vegetable stock
⅔ cup light cream
2 teaspoons cornstarch
salt and freshly ground black pepper
a little heavy cream or plain yogurt,
    to garnish
4 orange wedges, to serve

1 Soften the onion in the oil in a large pan. Add the watercress, unchopped, to the onion. Cover and cook for about 5 minutes until the watercress is soft.

2 Add the orange peel and juice and the stock to the watercress mixture. Bring to a boil, cover, and simmer for 10 to 15 minutes.

3 Purée the soup in a blender or food processor thoroughly, and strain if you want a smoother texture. Blend the cream with the cornstarch until no lumps remain. Stir into the soup, stirring until blended. Season to taste.

4 Slowly return the soup to a boil, stirring until just lightly thickened. Check the seasoning.

5 Serve the soup with a swirl of cream or yogurt, and a wedge of orange to squeeze in at the last moment.

6 If serving the soup chilled, thicken as above and leave to cool, before chilling in the refrigerator. Garnish with cream or yogurt and orange, as above.

Chilled Almond Soup

V

Unless you are prepared to spend time pounding all the ingredients for this soup by hand, a food processor is essential. Then you'll find this Spanish soup is simple to make and refreshing to eat on a hot day.

INGREDIENTS

Serves 6

4 ounces fresh white bread

3 cups cold water

1 cup blanched almonds

2 garlic cloves, sliced

5 tablespoons olive oil

1½ tablespoons sherry vinegar

salt and freshly ground black pepper

For the garnish

toasted slivered almonds

seedless green and black grapes, halved
   and peeled

1 Break the bread into a large plastic bowl and pour ⅔ cup of the water on top. Leave to stand for 5 minutes.

2 Put the almonds and garlic in a blender or food processor and process until finely ground. Blend in the soaked bread.

3 Gradually add the oil until the mixture forms a smooth paste. Add the sherry vinegar and remaining cold water and process until smooth.

4 Transfer to a bowl and season with salt and pepper, adding a little more water if the soup is too thick. Chill for at least 3 hours. Serve with the toasted almonds and grapes scattered on top.

Cucumber and Yogurt Soup with Walnuts

This is a particularly refreshing chilled soup, using a classic combination of cucumber and yogurt.

INGREDIENTS

Serves 5–6

1 cucumber

4 garlic cloves

½ teaspoon salt

¾ cup walnuts

1½ ounces day-old bread, torn into pieces

2 tablespoons walnut or sunflower oil

1⅔ cups plain yogurt

½ cup cold water or chilled still mineral water

1 to 2 teaspoons lemon juice

For the garnish

scant ½ cup coarsely chopped walnuts

1½ tablespoons olive oil

sprigs of fresh dill

3 When the mixture is smooth, slowly add the walnut or sunflower oil and combine well.

COOK'S TIP

If you prefer your soup smooth, purée it in a food processor or blender before serving.

---

4 Transfer the mixture into a large bowl and beat in the yogurt and diced cucumber. Add the cold water or mineral water and lemon juice to taste.

5 Pour the soup into chilled soup bowls to serve. Garnish with the chopped walnuts, drizzle with the olive oil, and arrange the sprigs of dill on top. Serve at once.

1 Cut the cucumber in half and peel one half of it. Dice the cucumber flesh; set aside.

2 Using a large mortar and pestle, crush together the garlic and salt. Add the walnuts and bread and continue working together.

V

Green Pea and Mint Soup

Perfect partners, peas and mint capture the flavors of summer.

INGREDIENTS

Serves 4

4 tablespoons butter

4 scallions, chopped

3 cups shelled fresh or frozen peas

2½ cups vegetable stock

2 large sprigs of fresh mint

2½ cups milk

a pinch of sugar (optional)

salt and freshly ground black pepper

small sprigs of fresh mint, to garnish

light cream, to serve

1 Melt the butter in a large saucepan. Add the chopped scallions and cook slowly over low heat until they are soft but not brown.

2 Stir the peas into the pan. Add the stock and mint and bring to a boil. Cover and simmer for about 30 minutes if you are using fresh peas (15 minutes if you are using frozen peas) until they are tender. Remove about 3 tablespoons of the peas, and reserve them to use for a garnish.

3 Pour the soup into a food processor or blender. Add the milk and purée until smooth. Season to taste, adding a pinch of sugar, if liked. Leave to cool, then chill lightly in the refrigerator.

4 Pour the soup into bowls. Swirl a little cream into each bowl. Garnish with the mint and the reserved peas, and serve.

Beet and Apricot Swirl

This soup is most attractive if you swirl together the two differently colored mixtures. If you prefer, however, they can be mixed together to save on both time and dishwashing.

INGREDIENTS

Serves 4

4 large cooked beets, roughly chopped

1 small onion, roughly chopped

2½ cups chicken stock

1 cup dried apricots

1 cup orange juice

salt and freshly ground black pepper

2 Place the rest of the onion in a pan with the apricots and orange juice. Cover and simmer for about 15 minutes until tender. Purée in a food processor or blender.

3 Return the 2 mixtures to the saucepans and reheat. Season each to taste with salt and pepper. To serve, swirl the mixture together in soup bowls to make a marbled effect.

1 Place the roughly chopped beets and half the onion in a pan with the stock. Bring to a boil. Lower the heat, cover, and simmer for about 10 minutes. Transfer to a food processor or blender and purée until smooth.

COOK'S TIP

The apricot mixture should be the same consistency as the beet mixture—if it is too thick, add a little extra orange juice.

V

Roasted Pepper Soup

Broiling intensifies the flavor of sweet red and yellow bell peppers and helps preserve the stunning color of this delicious soup.

INGREDIENTS

Serves 4

3 red bell peppers

1 yellow bell pepper

1 onion, chopped

1 garlic clove, crushed

3 cups vegetable stock

1 tablespoon all-purpose flour

salt and freshly ground black pepper

diced red and yellow bell peppers, to garnish

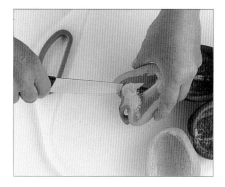

1 Heat the broiler. Cut the peppers in half. Remove the stems, cores, and all the white pith, and scrape out the seeds.

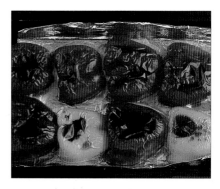

2 Line a broiler pan with foil and arrange the halved peppers, skin side up, in a single layer on the foil. Broil until the skins are black and blistered.

3 Transfer the peppers to a plastic bag and leave until cool. Peel off the skins and discard. Roughly chop the pepper flesh.

4 Put the onion, garlic clove, and ⅔ cup of the stock in a large saucepan. Boil for about 5 minutes until the stock reduces in volume. Lower the heat and stir until the onion and garlic are soft and just beginning to color.

5 Sprinkle the flour over the onion. Gradually stir in the remaining stock.

6 Add the chopped, roasted peppers. Bring to a boil. Cover the saucepan and simmer for 5 minutes longer.

7 Leave the soup to cool slightly, then purée in a food processor or blender until smooth. Season to taste with salt and ground black pepper. Return to the saucepan and reheat until piping hot.

8 Ladle into 4 soup bowls and garnish each with a sprinkling of diced peppers.

VARIATION
～

If you prefer, garnish the soup with a swirl of plain yogurt instead of the diced peppers.

Chicken Stellette Soup

*Easy and quick to prepare, especially
if you have good stock in the
refrigerator or freezer, this light,
clear soup is attractive to the palate
and the eye.*

INGREDIENTS

Serves 4 to 6

3¾ cups chicken stock

1 bay leaf

4 scallions, sliced

3 cups sliced white mushrooms

4-ounce cooked chicken breast half

½ cup small soup pasta (*stellette*)

⅔ cup dry white wine

1 tablespoon chopped fresh parsley

salt and freshly ground black pepper

1 Put the stock and bay leaf into a large saucepan and bring to a boil. Add the sliced scallions and mushrooms.

2 Remove the skin from the chicken and discard. Slice the chicken thinly. Add it to the soup and season to taste with salt and pepper. Heat through for 2 to 3 minutes.

3 Add the pasta to the soup, cover, and simmer for 7 to 8 minutes until the pasta is *al dente*.

4 Just before serving, add the wine and chopped parsley. Heat through again for 2 to 3 minutes. Pour into individual soup bowls and serve at once.

Zucchini Soup with Pasta

This is a pretty, fresh-tasting soup, which is always a welcome dish in hot weather.

INGREDIENTS

Serves 4 to 6

4 tablespoons olive or sunflower oil

2 onions, minced

1½ quarts chicken stock

2 pounds zucchini

1 cup small soup pasta (*stellette*)

a little lemon juice

2 tablespoons chopped fresh chervil

salt and freshly ground black pepper

sour cream, to serve

1 Heat the oil in a large saucepan. Add the onions, cover, and cook slowly for about 20 minutes, stirring occasionally, until soft but not colored.

2 Add the stock to the pan and bring the mixture to a boil.

3 Meanwhile, grate the zucchini and stir into the boiling stock with the pasta. Lower the heat, cover the pan, and simmer for 15 minutes until the pasta is tender.

4 Season to taste with lemon juice, and salt and pepper. Stir in the chopped fresh chervil. Pour into bowls and add a swirl of sour cream before serving.

VARIATION

Use cucumber instead of zucchini, if you prefer, and any shape soup pasta, such as tiny shells.

Jalapeño Soup

Chicken, chili and avocado are combined to make this simple but unusual soup.

INGREDIENTS

Serves 6

1½ quarts chicken stock

2 cooked boneless chicken breast halves, skinned and cut into large strips

1 drained canned jalapeño or chipotle chili, rinsed

1 avocado

COOK'S TIP

When using canned chilies, it is important to rinse them thoroughly before adding them to a dish to remove the flavor of any pickling liquid.

1 Heat the stock in a large saucepan. Add the chicken and chili and simmer over very low heat for 5 minutes to heat the chicken through and release the flavor from the chili.

2 Cut the avocado in half, remove the pit, and peel. Slice the avocado flesh lengthwise into neat strips.

3 Using a slotted spoon, remove the chili from the stock and discard. Pour the soup into warm serving bowls, distributing the chicken evenly between them.

4 Carefully add a few avocado slices to each bowl. Serve the soup at once while still hot.

Tamarind Soup with Peanuts and Vegetables

Lengkuas, also known as greater galangal, is a creamy colored ribizone from Southeast Asia. If you can't find it in Asian grocery stores, use a 2-inch piece of ginger root.

INGREDIENTS

Serves 4

5 shallots or 1 red onion, sliced

3 garlic cloves, crushed

1-inch piece lengkuas, peeled and sliced

1 or 2 fresh red chilies, seeded and sliced

¼ cup raw peanuts

½-inch cube shrimp paste, prepared

1¼ quarts well-flavored stock

½ to ¾ cup salted peanuts, lightly crushed

1 to 2 tablespoons dark brown sugar

1 teaspoon tamarind pulp, soaked in
    5 tablespoons warm water for
    15 minutes

salt

For the vegetables

1 chayote, thinly peeled, seeds removed,
    and flesh finely sliced

1 cup trimmed and finely sliced thin
    green beans

½ cup corn kernels (optional)

a handful of green leaves, such as
    watercress, aragula, or Napa cabbage,
    finely shredded

1 fresh green chili, sliced, to garnish

1 Grind the shallots or onion, garlic, lengkuas, chilies, raw peanuts, and shrimp paste to a paste in a food processor, or use a mortar and pestle.

2 Pour in some of the stock to moisten. Pour this mixture into a pan or wok, adding the rest of the stock. Add the crushed salted peanuts and sugar and cook for 15 minutes.

3 Strain the tamarind pulp, discarding the seeds; reserve the juice.

4 About 5 minutes before serving, add the chayote slices, beans, and corn kernels, if using, to the soup and boil rapidly. At the last minute, add the green leaves and salt to taste.

5 Add the tamarind juice and adjust the seasoning. Serve at once, garnished with slices of green chili.

Spinach and Tofu Soup

Serve this extremely delicate and mild-flavored soup to counterbalance the heat from a hot Thai curry. Look for dried shrimp and fish sauce in Asian grocery stores.

INGREDIENTS

Serves 4 to 6

2 tablespoons dried shrimp

1 quart chicken stock

1½ cups fresh firm tofu, drained and cut into ¾-inch cubes

2 tablespoons fish sauce

12 ounces fresh spinach

freshly ground black pepper

2 scallions, finely sliced, to garnish

1 Rinse and drain the dried shrimp. Combine the shrimp with the chicken stock in a large saucepan and bring to a boil. Add the tofu and simmer for about 5 minutes. Season with fish sauce and black pepper to taste.

2 Rinse the spinach leaves thoroughly and tear into bite-size pieces. Add to the soup. Simmer for 1 to 2 minutes longer.

3 Pour the soup into warm bowls. Sprinkle the chopped scallions on top to garnish, and serve.

Chinese Tofu and Lettuce Soup

V

This light, clear soup is brimming with colorful, flavorsome vegetables.

INGREDIENTS

Serves 4

2 tablespoons peanut or sunflower oil

1½ cups cubed smoked or marinated firm tofu

3 scallions, sliced diagonally

2 garlic cloves, cut into thin strips

1 carrot, finely sliced

1 quart vegetable stock

2 tablespoons soy sauce

l tablespoon dry sherry or vermouth

1 teaspoon sugar

2 cups shredded Romaine lettuce

salt and freshly ground black pepper

1 Heat the oil in a hot wok. Add the tofu cubes and stir-fry until they are brown. Drain on paper towels; set aside.

2 Add the scallions, garlic, and carrot to the wok. Stir-fry for 2 minutes. Add the stock, soy sauce, sherry or vermouth, sugar, lettuce, and fried tofu. Heat through for 1 minute over low heat. Season to taste, and serve.

Chinese Chicken and Asparagus Soup

This is a very delicate and delicious soup. When fresh asparagus is not in season, canned white asparagus is an acceptable substitute.

INGREDIENTS

Serves 4

5-ounce boneless chicken breast half, skinned

pinch of salt

1 teaspoon egg white

1 teaspoon cornstarch paste

4 ounces asparagus

3 cups chicken stock

salt and freshly ground black pepper

fresh cilantro leaves, to garnish

1 Cut the chicken meat into thin slices, each about the size of a postage stamp. Mix with a pinch of salt, then add the egg white and cornstarch paste.

2 Cut off and discard the tough ends of the asparagus. Diagonally cut the tender spears into short, even pieces.

3 In a wok or saucepan, bring the stock to a rolling boil. Add the asparagus, return to a boil and cook for 2 minutes: You do not need to do this if you are using canned asparagus.

4 Add the chicken, stir to separate and bring back to a boil. Adjust the seasonings. Serve hot, garnished with fresh cilantro leaves.

Hot-and-Sour Shrimp Soup with Lemongrass

This classic seafood soup, known as Tom Yam Goong, is probably the most popular and best-known soup from Thailand.

INGREDIENTS

Serves 4 to 6

1 pound jumbo shrimp

1 quart chicken stock or water

3 lemongrass stalks

10 kaffir lime leaves, torn in half

8-ounce can straw mushrooms, drained

3 tablespoons fish sauce

4 tablespoons lime juice

2 tablespoons chopped scallions

1 tablespoon fresh cilantro leaves

4 fresh red chilies, seeded and chopped

2 scallions, minced, to garnish

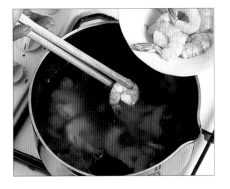

3 Strain the stock into a bowl. Return it to the saucepan and reheat. Add the mushrooms and shrimp and cook until the shrimp are pink.

4 Stir in the fish sauce, lime juice, scallions, cilantro, red chilies, and the remaining lime leaves. Taste and adjust the seasoning: The soup should be sour, salty, spicy, and hot. Garnish with finely chopped scallions before serving.

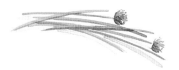

1 Shell and devein the shrimps, set aside. Rinse the shrimp shells and place in a large saucepan with the stock or water and bring to a boil.

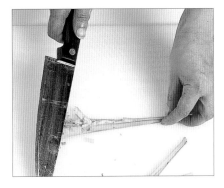

2 Bruise the lemongrass stalks with the blunt edge of a chopping knife and add them to the stock, together with half the lime leaves. Simmer for 5 to 6 minutes until the stalks change color and the stock is fragrant.

Duck Consommé

The Vietnamese community in France has had a profound influence on French cooking, as this soup bears witness—it is light and rich at the same time, with intriguing flavors of Southeast Asia.

INGREDIENTS

Serves 4

1 duck carcass (raw or cooked), plus 2 legs or any giblets, trimmed of as much fat as possible

1 large onion, unpeeled, with the root end trimmed

2 carrots, cut into 2-inch pieces

1 parsnip, cut into 2-inch pieces

1 leek, cut into 2-inch pieces

2 to 4 garlic cloves, crushed

1-inch piece fresh ginger root, peeled and sliced

1 tablespoon black peppercorns

4 to 6 sprigs of fresh thyme, or 1 teaspoon dried thyme

6 to 8 sprigs of cilantro, leaves and stems separated

For the garnish

1 small carrot

1 small leek, halved lengthwise

4 to 6 shiitake mushrooms, thinly sliced

soy sauce

2 scallions, thinly sliced

watercress or finely shredded Napa cabbage leaves

freshly ground black pepper

1 Put the duck carcass and legs or giblets, onion, carrots, parsnip, leek, and garlic in a large, heavy saucepan or flameproof casserole. Add the ginger, peppercorns, thyme, and cilantro stems. Cover with cold water and bring to a boil over medium-high heat, skimming any foam from the surface.

2 Lower the heat and simmer for 1½ to 2 hours. Strain through a cheesecloth-lined strainer into a bowl, discarding the bones and vegetables. Cool the stock and chill for several hours or overnight. Skim off any congealed fat and blot the surface with paper towels to remove any traces of fat.

3 To make the garnish, cut the carrot and leek into 2-inch pieces. Cut each piece lengthwise in thin slices. Stack and slice the thin slices into thin julienne strips. Place in a large saucepan with the sliced mushrooms.

4 Pour the stock over and add a few dashes of soy sauce and some pepper. Bring to a boil over medium-high heat, skimming any foam from the surface. Adjust the seasoning. Stir in the scallions and watercress or Napa cabbage leaves. Ladle the consommé into warm bowls and sprinkle with the cilantro leaves before serving.

Pork and Pickled Mustard Greens Soup

Look for Sichuan-style pickled mustard greens leaves in Chinese grocery stores.

INGREDIENTS

Serves 4 to 6

8 ounces pickled mustard greens leaves

2 ounces cellophane noodles, soaked

1 tablespoon vegetable oil

4 garlic cloves, finely sliced

1 quart chicken stock

1 pound pork spareribs, cut into large chunks

2 tablespoons fish sauce

a pinch of sugar

freshly ground black pepper

2 fresh chilies, seeded and finely sliced, to
　garnish

1 Soak the pickled mustard leaves before cutting into bite-size pieces. If they are too salty, soak them for a little longer.

2 Drain the cellophane noodles, discarding the soaking water. Cut the noodles into pieces about 2 inches long.

3 Heat the oil in a small skillet. Add the garlic and stir-fry until golden. Transfer to a bowl; set aside.

4 Put the stock in a saucepan and bring to a boil. Add the spareribs and simmer for 10 to 15 minutes.

5 Add the pickled mustard leaves and cellophane noodles. Return to a boil. Season to taste with fish sauce, sugar, and freshly ground black pepper.

6 Pour the soup into serving bowls. Garnish with the fried garlic and the chilies. Serve piping hot.

RICH &
CREAMY SOUPS

V

Broccoli and Almond Soup

The creaminess of the toasted almonds combines perfectly with the slightly bitter taste of the broccoli.

INGREDIENTS

Serves 4 to 6

½ cup blanched almonds, very finely
    ground

1½ pounds broccoli

3¾ cups vegetable stock or water

1¼ cups skim milk

salt and freshly ground black pepper

1 Heat the oven to 350°F. Spread the ground almonds evenly on a cookie sheet and toast in the oven for about 10 minutes until golden. Reserve one-quarter of the almonds to sprinkle over the finished dish.

2 Cut the broccoli into small flowerets and steam for 6 to 7 minutes until tender.

3 Place the remaining toasted almonds, broccoli, stock or water, and milk in a blender and blend until smooth. Season with salt and pepper to taste.

4 Reheat the soup and serve sprinkled with the reserved toasted almonds.

Broccoli and Stilton Soup

This is a really easy but rich soup—choose something simple to follow, such as plainly roasted or broiled meat, poultry, or fish.

INGREDIENTS

Serves 4

12 ounces broccoli

2 tablespoons butter

1 onion, chopped

1 leek, white part only, chopped

1 small potato, cut into chunks

2½ cups chicken stock, hot

1¼ cups milk

3 tablespoons heavy cream

4 ounces Stilton cheese, rind removed, crumbled

salt and freshly ground black pepper

1 Break the broccoli into flowerets, discarding any tough stems. Set aside 2 small flowerets to garnish the finished dish.

2 Melt the butter in a large pan. Add the onion and leek and fry until soft but not colored. Add the broccoli and potato, and pour in the stock. Cover and simmer for 15 to 20 minutes until the vegetables are tender.

3 Leave the soup to cool slightly. Pour into a blender or food processor and purée until smooth. Pour the mixture through a strainer back into the rinsed pan.

4 Add the milk and heavy cream to the pan. Season to taste with salt and freshly ground black pepper. Reheat slowly. At the last minute add the cheese, stirring until it just melts: Do not boil.

5 Meanwhile, blanch the reserved broccoli flowerets and cut them vertically into thin slices. Ladle the soup into warm bowls and garnish with the sliced broccoli and a generous grinding of black pepper.

Tomato and Blue Cheese Soup

The concentrated flavor of roasted tomatoes strikes a great balance with strong blue cheese.

INGREDIENTS

Serves 4

3 pounds ripe tomatoes, peeled, quartered, and seeded

2 garlic cloves, minced

2 tablespoons vegetable oil or butter

1 leek, chopped

1 carrot, chopped

1¼ quarts unsalted chicken stock

4 ounces blue cheese, crumbled

3 tablespoons whipping cream

several large fresh basil leaves, or 1 to 2 fresh parsley sprigs, plus extra, to garnish

1 cup cooked and crumbled bacon, to garnish

salt and freshly ground black pepper

1 Heat the oven to 400°F. Spread the tomatoes in a shallow baking dish. Sprinkle with the garlic and some salt and pepper. Place in the oven and roast for 35 minutes.

2 Heat the oil or butter in a large saucepan. Add the leek and carrot and season lightly with salt and pepper. Cook over low heat, stirring often, for about 10 minutes until soft.

3 Stir in the stock and roasted tomatoes. Bring to a boil. Lower the heat, cover, and simmer for about 20 minutes.

4 Add the blue cheese, cream, and basil or parsley. Transfer to a food processor or blender and process until smooth, working in batches if necessary. Taste and adjust the seasoning.

5 Reheat the soup, but do not boil. Serve garnished with bacon and a sprig of fresh herbs.

Cauliflower and Walnut Cream Soup

Even though there isn't any cream added to this soup, the cauliflower gives it a delicious, rich, creamy texture.

INGREDIENTS

Serves 4

1 medium cauliflower

1 onion, roughly chopped

scant 2 cups chicken or vegetable stock

scant 2 cups skim milk

3 tablespoons walnuts

salt and freshly ground black pepper

paprika and chopped walnuts, to garnish

1 Trim off the the cauliflower's outer leaves and break into small flowerets. Place the cauliflower, onion and stock in a large saucepan.

2 Bring to a boil. Cover and simmer for about 15 minutes until soft. Add the milk and walnuts. Purée in a blender or food processor until smooth.

3 Season the soup to taste with salt and pepper. Reheat and return to a boil. Serve sprinkled with a dusting of paprika and chopped walnuts.

VARIATION

If you prefer, make this soup using broccoli instead of cauliflower. Or use almonds instead of walnuts.

Carrot and Coriander Soup

Use a good homemade stock for this soup—it adds a far greater depth of flavor than stock made from cubes.

INGREDIENTS

Serves 4

4 tablespoons butter

3 leeks, sliced

3 cups sliced carrots

1 tablespoon ground coriander

1¼ quarts chicken stock

⅔ cup thick plain yogurt

salt and freshly ground black pepper

2–3 tablespoons chopped fresh cilantro, to garnish

3 Leave to cool slightly. Purée the soup in a blender until smooth. Return the soup to the rinsed pan and add 2 tablespoons of the yogurt. Taste the soup and adjust the seasoning. Reheat slowly. Do not boil.

4 Ladle the soup into bowls and put a spoonful of the remaining yogurt in the center of each. Scatter the chopped cilantro over and serve at once.

1 Melt the butter in a large pan. Add the leeks and carrots and stir well. Cover and cook for 10 minutes until the vegetables are beginning to become soft.

2 Stir in the ground coriander and cook for about 1 minute. Pour in the stock and add seasoning to taste. Bring to a boil. Lower the heat, cover, and simmer for about 20 minutes until the leeks and carrots are tender.

Carrot Soup with Ginger

The zing of fresh ginger root is an ideal complement to the sweetness of cooked carrots.

INGREDIENTS

Serves 6

2 tablespoons butter or margarine

1 onion, chopped

1 celery stalk, chopped

1 medium potato, chopped

5½ cups chopped carrots

2 teaspoons minced fresh ginger root

1½ quarts chicken stock

7 tablespoons whipping cream

a good pinch of freshly grated nutmeg

salt and freshly ground black pepper

1 Melt the butter or margarine. Add the onion and celery and cook for about 5 minutes until soft.

2 Stir in the potato, carrots, ginger, and stock. Bring to a boil. Lower the heat to low, cover, and simmer for about 20 minutes.

3 Pour the soup into a food processor or blender and process until it is smooth. Alternatively, use a vegetable mill to purée the soup. Return the soup to the pan. Stir in the cream and nutmeg and add salt and pepper to taste. Reheat slowly to serve.

Jerusalem Artichoke Soup

Topped with saffron cream, this soup is wonderful on a chilly day.

INGREDIENTS

Serves 4

4 tablespoons butter

1 onion, chopped

3¼ cups peeled and chopped
   Jerusalem artichokes

3¾ cups chicken stock

⅔ cup milk

⅔ cup heavy cream

a good pinch of saffron powder

salt and freshly ground black pepper

snipped fresh chives, to garnish

1 Melt the butter in a large, heavy-bottomed pan. Add the onion and fry for 5 to 8 minutes until soft but not brown, stirring from time to time.

2 Add the Jeruslaem artichokes to the pan and stir until coated in the butter. Cover and cook slowly for 10 to 15 minutes, being careful not to let the artichokes turn brown. Pour in the chicken stock and milk. Recover and simmer for 15 minutes. Cool slightly, then process in a blender or food processor until smooth.

3 Strain the soup back into the rinsed pan. Add half the cream, season to taste, and reheat slowly. Lightly whip the remaining cream and the saffron powder. Ladle the soup into warm soup bowls and put a spoonful of saffron cream in the center of each. Scatter the snipped chives over the top and serve at once.

Spiced Parsnip Soup

This pale, creamy-textured soup is given a special touch with an aromatic, spiced garlic-and-mustard-seed garnish.

INGREDIENTS

Serves 4 to 6

3 tablespoons butter

1 onion, chopped

5½ cups diced parsnips

1 teaspoon ground coriander

½ teaspoon ground cumin

½ teaspoon turmeric

¼ teaspoon cayenne pepper

5 cups chicken stock

⅔ cup light cream

1 tablespoon sunflower oil

1 garlic clove, cut into julienne strips

2 teaspoons yellow mustard seeds

salt and freshly ground black pepper

1 Melt the butter in a large pan. Add the onion and parsnips and fry slowly for about 3 minutes.

2 Stir in the spices and cook for 1 minute longer. Add the stock, season with salt and pepper, and bring to a boil.

3 Lower the heat, cover, and simmer for about 45 minutes until the parsnips are tender. Cool slightly, then purée in a blender or food processor until smooth. Return the soup to the rinsed pan. Add the cream and heat through slowly over low heat.

4 Heat the oil in a small pan. Add the julienne strips of garlic and the yellow mustard seeds and fry quickly until the garlic is beginning to brown and the mustard seeds start to pop and splutter. Remove from the heat.

5 Ladle the soup into warm soup bowls and pour a little of the hot spice mixture over each. Serve at once.

Moroccan Vegetable Soup

Creamy parsnip and pumpkin give this soup a wonderfully rich texture.

INGREDIENTS

Serves 4

1 tablespoon olive or sunflower oil

1 tablespoon butter

1 onion, chopped

1½ cups chopped carrots

1½ cups chopped parsnips

8 ounces pumpkin

about 3¾ cups vegetable or chicken stock

lemon juice, to taste

salt and freshly ground black pepper

For the garnish

1½ teaspoons olive oil

½ garlic clove, minced

3 tablespoons chopped fresh parsley and
    cilantro, mixed

a good pinch of paprika

1 Heat the oil and butter in a large pan. Add the onion and fry for about 3 minutes until soft, stirring occasionally. Add the carrots and parsnips and stir well. Cover and cook over low heat for 5 minutes longer.

2 Cut the pumpkin into chunks, discarding the skin and pith. Stir into the pan, cover, and cook for 5 minutes longer. Add the stock and seasoning and slowly bring to a boil. Cover and simmer for 35 to 40 minutes until the vegetables are tender.

3 Leave the soup to cool slightly. Pour into a food processor or blender and purée until smooth, adding a little extra water if the soup seems too thick. Pour back into the rinsed pan and reheat slowly.

4 To make the garnish, heat the oil in a small pan. Add the garlic and herbs and fry for 1 to 2 minutes. Add the paprika and stir well.

5 Adjust the seasoning of the soup and stir in lemon juice to taste. Pour into bowls and spoon a little of the prepared garnish on top, which should then be lightly swirled into the soup.

Creamy Zucchini and Dolcelatte Soup

V

The beauty of this soup is its delicate color, its creamy texture, and its subtle taste. If you prefer a more pronounced cheese flavor, use gorgonzola instead of dolcelatte.

INGREDIENTS

Serves 4 to 6

2 tablespoons olive oil

1 tablespoon butter

1 onion, roughly chopped

6 cups trimmed and sliced zucchini

1 teaspoon dried oregano

about 2½ cups vegetable stock

4 ounces dolcelatte cheese, rind
   removed, diced

1¼ cups light cream

salt and freshly ground black pepper

To garnish

sprigs of fresh oregano

extra dolcelatte cheese

1 Heat the oil and butter in a large saucepan until foaming. Add the onion and cook slowly for about 5 minutes, stirring frequently, until soft but not brown.

2 Add the zucchini and oregano, with salt and pepper to taste. Cook over medium heat for 10 minutes, stirring frequently.

3 Pour in the stock and bring to a boil, stirring frequently. Lower the heat, half-cover the pan, and simmer, stirring occasionally, for about 30 minutes. Stir in the diced dolcelatte until it melts.

4 Process the soup in a blender or food processor until smooth. Press through a strainer into the rinsed pan.

5 Add two-thirds of the cream and stir over low heat until hot, but not boiling. Check the consistency and add more stock if the soup is too thick. Taste and adjust seasoning if necessary.

6 Pour into warm bowls. Swirl in the remaining cream, garnish with fresh oregano and extra crumbled dolcelatte cheese. Serve at once.

V

Fresh Pea Soup St. Germain

This soup takes its name from a suburb of Paris where peas used to be cultivated in market gardens.

Serves 2 to 3

a small knob of butter

2 or 3 shallots, minced

3 cups shelled fresh peas (from about 3 pounds garden peas)

2¼ cups water

3 to 4 tablespoons whipping cream (optional)

salt and freshly ground black pepper

croutons, to garnish

3 When the peas are tender, ladle them into a food processor or blender with a little of the cooking liquid and process until smooth.

4 Strain the soup into the rinsed saucepan or casserole. Stir in the cream, if using. Heat through without boiling. Add the seasoning and serve hot, garnished with croutons.

COOK'S TIP

∾

If fresh peas are not available, use frozen peas, but thaw and rinse them before use.

1 Melt the butter in a heavy-bottomed saucepan or flameproof casserole. Add the shallots and cook for about 3 minutes, stirring occasionally.

2 Add the peas and water and season with salt and a little pepper. Cover and simmer for about 12 minutes for young peas and up to 18 minutes for large or older peas, stirring occasionally.

Green Bean and Parmesan Soup

V

Fresh green beans and Parmesan cheese make a simple but delicious combination of flavors.

INGREDIENTS

Serves 4

2 tablespoons butter or margarine

8 ounces green beans, trimmed

1 garlic clove, crushed

scant 2 cups vegetable stock

½ cup grated Parmesan cheese

¼ cup light cream

salt and freshly ground black pepper

2 tablespoons chopped fresh parsley, to garnish

1 Melt the butter or margarine in a medium saucepan. Add the green beans and garlic and cook for 2 to 3 minutes over medium heat, stirring frequently.

2 Stir in the stock and season with salt and pepper. Bring to a boil. Lower the heat and simmer, uncovered, for 10 to 15 minutes until the beans are tender.

3 Pour the soup into a blender or food processor and process until smooth. Alternatively, purée the soup in a food mill. Return to the pan and reheat slowly.

4 Stir in the Parmesan cheese and cream and sprinkle with the parsley. Serve hot.

V

Cream of Spinach Soup

This is a deliciously creamy soup you will find yourself making over and over again.

INGREDIENTS

Serves 4

2 tablespoons butter

1 small onion, chopped

1½ pounds fresh spinach, chopped

1¼ quarts vegetable stock

2 ounces creamed coconut

freshly grated nutmeg

1¼ cups light cream

salt and freshly ground black pepper

fresh snipped chives, to garnish

3 Return the mixture to the rinsed pan. Add the remaining stock and the creamed coconut, with salt, pepper, and nutmeg to taste. Simmer for 15 minutes to thicken.

4 Add the cream to the pan, stir well, and heat through. Do not boil. Serve hot, garnished with long strips of chives.

1 Melt the butter in a saucepan over medium heat. Add the onion and sauté for a few minutes until soft. Add the spinach, cover, the pan, and cook slowly for 10 minutes until the spinach wilts and reduces.

2 Pour the spinach mixture into a blender or food processor and add a little of the stock. Blend until smooth.

Watercress Soup

V

*A delicious and nutritious soup,
which is best served with
crusty bread.*

INGREDIENTS

Serves 4

1 tablespoon sunflower oil

1 tablespoon butter

1 onion, minced

1 potato, diced

about 6 ounces watercress

1¾ cups vegetable stock

1¾ cups milk

lemon juice, to taste

salt and freshly ground black pepper

sour cream, to serve

1 Heat the oil and butter in a
large saucepan. Add the onion
and fry over low heat until soft but
not brown. Add the potato and fry
slowly for 2 to 3 minutes. Cover
and sweat for 5 minutes over low
heat, stirring from time to time.

2 Strip the watercress leaves
from the stems and roughly
chop the stems.

COOK'S TIP

If you leave out
the sour cream, this is
a low-calorie soup.

---

3 Add the stock and milk to the
pan and stir in the chopped
stems. Season and bring to a boil.
Simmer, partially covered, for
10 to 12 minutes until the potatoes
are tender. Add all but a few of the
watercress leaves and simmer for
2 minutes longer.

4 Process the soup in a food
processor or blender. Return
to the saucepan and heat slowly
with the reserved watercress leaves.

5 Taste the soup when hot, add
a little lemon juice and adjust
the seasoning.

6 Pour the soup into warm soup
bowls. Garnish with a little
sour cream in the center just
before serving.

Cream of Avocado Soup

*Avocados make wonderful soup—
pretty, delicious, and refreshing.*

INGREDIENTS

Serves 4

2 large ripe avocados

1 quart chicken stock

1 cup light cream

salt and freshly ground white pepper

1 tablespoon minced fresh cilantro leaves,
    to garnish (optional)

1 Cut the avocados in half,
remove the pits, and mash the
flesh. Put the flesh into a nylon
strainer and press it through the
strainer with a wooden spoon into
a warm soup bowl.

2 Heat the chicken stock with
the cream in a saucepan.
When the mixture is hot, but not
boiling, whisk it into the puréed
avocado in the bowl.

3 Season to taste with salt and
pepper. Serve immediately,
sprinkled with the cilantro, if
using. The soup may be served
chilled, if preferred.

Cream of Red Pepper Soup

Broiling bell peppers gives them a sweet, smoky flavor, which is delicious in salads or, as here, in a velvety soup with a secret flavoring of rosemary to add aromatic depth. The soup is equally good served hot or chilled, as you prefer.

INGREDIENTS

Serves 4

4 red bell peppers

2 tablespoons butter

1 onion, minced

1 sprig of fresh rosemary

1¼ quarts chicken or light vegetable stock

3 tablespoons tomato paste

½ cup heavy cream

paprika

salt and freshly ground black pepper

1 Heat the broiler. Put the peppers in the broiler pan under high heat and turn them regularly until the skins blacken all around. Put them into plastic bags and close. Leave for 20 minutes.

2 Peel the black skin off the peppers. Avoid rinsing them because this loses some of the natural oil and hence the flavor.

3 Halve the peppers, removing the seeds, stems and pith. Roughly chop the flesh.

4 Melt the butter in a deep saucepan. Add the onion and rosemary and cook slowly over low heat for about 5 minutes. Remove the rosemary and discard.

5 Add the peppers and stock to the onion and bring to a boil. Simmer for 15 minutes. Stir in the tomato paste. Process or strain the soup to a smooth purée.

6 Stir in half the cream and season with paprika, salt, if necessary, and pepper.

7 Serve the soup hot or chilled, with the remaining cream swirled delicately on top. Speckle the cream very lightly with a pinch of paprika.

Creamy Tomato Soup

Tomato soup is an old favorite. This version is made special by the addition of fresh herbs and cream.

INGREDIENTS

Serves 4

2 tablespoons butter or margarine

1 onion, chopped

2 pounds tomatoes, peeled and quartered

2 carrots, chopped

2 cups chicken stock

2 tablespoons chopped fresh parsley

½ teaspoon fresh thyme leaves, plus extra
   to garnish

5 tablespoons whipping cream (optional)

salt and freshly ground black pepper

1 Melt the butter or margarine in a large saucepan. Add the onion and cook for 5 minutes until soft.

2 Stir in the tomatoes, carrots, chicken stock, parsley, and thyme. Bring to a boil. Lower the heat to low, cover the pan, and simmer for 15 to 20 minutes until the vegetables are tender.

3 Purée the soup in a vegetable mill until smooth. Return the puréed soup to the saucepan.

4 Stir in the cream, if using, and reheat slowly. Season the soup to taste with salt and freshly ground black pepper. Ladle into warm soup bowls and serve piping hot, garnished with fresh thyme leaves.

COOK'S TIP

Meaty and flavorful, plum tomatoes are the best choice for this traditional soup.

Cream of Scallion Soup

V

The oniony flavor of this soup is surprisingly delicate.

INGREDIENTS

Serves 4 to 6

2 tablespoons butter

1 small onion, chopped

1¾ cups chopped scallions

1½ cups peeled and chopped potatoes

2½ cups vegetable stock

1½ cups light cream

2 tablespoons lemon juice

salt and freshly ground white pepper

chopped scallion greens or fresh chives, to garnish

1 Melt the butter in a saucepan. Add the onion and scallions, cover, and cook over very low heat for about 10 minutes, or until soft.

2 Add the potatoes and the stock and bring to a boil. Cover again and simmer over medium-low heat for about 30 minutes. Cool slightly.

3 Purée the soup in a blender or food processor.

4 If serving the soup hot, pour it back into the rinsed pan. Add the cream and season with salt and pepper. Reheat slowly, stirring occasionally. Add the lemon juice.

5 If serving the soup cold, pour it into a bowl. Stir in the cream and lemon juice and season with salt and pepper. Cover the bowl and chill for at least 1 hour.

6 Sprinkle with the chopped scallion greens or chives before serving.

[V]

Cream of Celery Root and Spinach Soup

Celery root has a wonderful flavor that is reminiscent of celery, but also has a slightly nutty taste. Here it is combined with spinach to make a delicious soup.

INGREDIENTS

Serves 6

1 quart water

1 cup dry white wine

1 leek, thickly sliced

3½ cups celery root, diced

7 ounces fresh spinach leaves

freshly grated nutmeg

salt and freshly ground black pepper

¼ cup pine nuts, to garnish

1 Combine the water and wine. Place the leek, celery root, and spinach in a deep saucepan and pour the liquid over the top. Bring to a boil, lower the heat, and simmer for 10 to 15 minutes until the vegetables are soft.

2 Pour the vegetables and liquid into a blender or food processor and purée, in batches if necessary, until smooth. Return to the rinsed pan and season to taste with salt, ground black pepper and nutmeg. Reheat slowly.

3 Heat a nonstick skillet (do not add any oil). Add the pine nuts and toast until golden brown, stirring occasionally so they do not stick. Sprinkle them over the soup and serve.

COOK'S TIP

If the soup is too thick, thin with a little water or 2% milk when puréeing.

Fresh Mushroom Soup with Tarragon

This is a light mushroom soup, subtly flavored with tarragon.

INGREDIENTS

Serves 6

1 tablespoon butter or margarine

4 shallots, minced

6 cups minced cremini mushrooms

1¼ cups vegetable stock

1¼ cups 2% milk

1 to 2 tablespoons chopped fresh tarragon

2 tablespoons dry sherry (optional)

salt and freshly ground black pepper

sprigs of fresh tarragon, to garnish

1 Melt the butter or margarine in a large saucepan. Add the shallots and cook over low heat for 5 minutes, stirring occasionally. Add the mushrooms and cook gently for 3 minutes, stirring. Add the stock and milk.

2 Bring to a boil. Lower the heat, cover, and simmer for about 20 minutes until the vegetables are soft. Stir in the chopped tarragon and season to taste with salt and pepper.

3 Leave the soup to cool slightly, then purée in a blender or food processor, in batches if necessary, until smooth. Return to the rinsed saucepan and reheat slowly.

4 Stir in the sherry, if using. Ladle the soup into warm soup bowls and serve garnished with sprigs of tarragon.

VARIATION

If you prefer, use a mixture of wild and white mushrooms rather than cremini.

Cream of Mushroom Soup

V

A good mushroom soup makes the most of the subtle and sometimes rather elusive flavor of mushrooms. White mushrooms are used here for their pale color; cremini or, better still, portobello mushrooms give a fuller flavor, but turn the soup brown.

INGREDIENTS

Serves 4

10 ounces white mushrooms
1 tablespoon sunflower oil
3 tablespoons butter
1 small onion, minced
1 tablespoon all-purpose flour
2 cups vegetable stock
2 cups milk
a pinch of dried basil
2 to 3 tablespoons light cream (optional)
salt and freshly ground black pepper
fresh basil leaves, to garnish

1 Separate the mushroom caps from the stems. Finely slice the caps and finely chop the stems.

2 Heat the oil and half the butter in a heavy-bottomed saucepan. Add the onion, mushroom stems and about three-quarters of the sliced mushroom caps. Fry for 1 to 2 minutes, stirring frequently. Cover the pan and sweat over low heat for 6 to 7 minutes, stirring from time to time.

3 Stir in the flour and cook for about 1 minute. Gradually add the stock and milk, to make a smooth, thin sauce. Add the dried basil and season to taste. Bring to a boil. Lower the heat and simmer, partly covered, for 15 minutes.

4 Cool the soup slightly. Pour into a food processor or blender and process until smooth. Melt the rest of the butter in a skillet. Add the remaining mushroom caps and fry over low heat for 3 to 4 minutes until they are just tender.

5 Pour the soup into the rinsed saucepan and stir in the fried mushrooms. Heat until very hot and adjust the seasoning. Add the cream, if using. Serve sprinkled with fresh basil leaves.

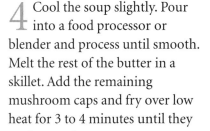

Balinese Vegetable Soup

V

Any seasonal vegetables can be used in this soup, which is known as Sayur Oelih in Bali.

INGREDIENTS

Serves 8

8 ounces green beans

1¼ quarts boiling water

1⅔ cups coconut milk

1 garlic clove

2 macadamia nuts or 4 almonds

½-inch cube shrimp paste

2 to 3 teaspoons coriander seeds,
    dry-fried and ground

oil for frying

1 onion, finely sliced

2 duan salam or bay leaves

8 ounces bean sprouts

2 tablespoons lemon juice

salt

1 Top and tail the green beans and cut into small pieces. Cook the beans in the salted, boiling water for 3 to 4 minutes. Drain the beans and reserve the cooking water.

2 Spoon off 3 to 4 tablespoons of the cream from the top of the coconut milk; set aside.

3 Grind the garlic, nuts, shrimp paste and ground coriander to a paste in a food processor or with a mortar and pestle.

4 Heat the oil in a wok or saucepan. Add the onion and fry until transparent. Remove from the pan and reserve. Fry the paste for 2 minutes without browning. Pour in the reserved bean cooking water and the coconut milk. Bring to a boil. Add the duan salam or bay leaves and cook, uncovered, for 15 to 20 minutes.

5 Just before serving, add the beans, fried onion, bean sprouts, reserved coconut cream, and lemon juice. Taste and adjust the seasoning, if necessary. Serve at once.

V

Yogurt Soup

Made from ground chick-peas, gram flour is sold in Asian groceries.

INGREDIENTS

Serves 4 to 6

2 cups plain yogurt, beaten

¼ cup gram flour (besan)

½ teaspoon cayenne pepper

½ teaspoon turmeric

salt, to taste

2 or 3 fresh green chilies, minced

4 tablespoons vegetable oil

1 whole dried red chili

1 teaspoon cumin seeds

3 or 4 curry leaves

3 garlic cloves, crushed

2-inch piece fresh ginger root, peeled and crushed

2 tablespoons chopped fresh cilantro

1 Mix together the yogurt, flour, cayenne and turmeric, and salt and pass through a strainer into a saucepan. Add the green chilies and simmer for about 10 minutes, stirring occasionally. Be careful not to let the soup boil over.

2 Heat the oil in a skillet. Add the remaining spices and fry with the garlic and ginger until the dried chili turns black. Stir in 1 tablespoon of the chopped fresh cilantro.

3 Pour the spices over the yogurt soup, cover the pan, and leave to rest for 5 minutes. Stir well and gently reheat for 5 minutes longer. Serve hot, garnished with the remaining chopped cilantro.

Egg and Cheese Soup

In this classic Roman soup, eggs and cheese are beaten into hot broth, producing a slightly "curdled" texture, which is a characteristic of the dish.

INGREDIENTS

Serves 6

3 eggs

3 tablespoons fine semolina

6 tablespoons grated Parmesan cheese

a pinch of freshly grated nutmeg

1½ quarts meat or chicken stock

salt and freshly ground black pepper

12 slices French bread, to serve

1 Beat the eggs in a bowl with the semolina and cheese. Add the nutmeg. Beat in 1 cup of the cool stock.

2 Meanwhile, heat the leftover stock to simmering point in a large saucepan.

3 When the stock is hot, whisk the egg mixture into the stock. Increase the heat slightly and bring it barely to a boil. Season with salt and pepper. Cook for 3 to 4 minutes: As the egg cooks, the soup will lose its smooth consistency.

4 To serve, toast the slices of French bread and place 2 of them in the bottom of each soup bowl. Ladle the hot soup on top of the bread and serve at once.

Creamy Corn Soup

This is simple to prepare, yet full of flavor. It is sometimes made with sour cream and cream cheese. Poblano chilies may be added for a fiery, authentic Mexican flavor.

Serves 4

2 tablespoons corn oil

1 onion, minced

1 red bell pepper, seeded and chopped

²/₃ cups whole corn kernels, thawed
    if frozen

3 cups chicken stock

1 cup light cream

salt and freshly ground black pepper

¹/₂ red bell pepper, seeded and finely
    diced, to garnish

3 Transfer the mixture to a saucepan and stir in the stock and salt and pepper to taste. Bring to a simmer and cook for 5 minutes.

4 Slowly stir in the cream. Serve the soup hot or chilled, sprinkled with the diced red pepper. If serving hot, reheat slowly after adding the cream. Do not let the soup boil.

1 Heat the oil in a skillet. Add the onion and red pepper and sauté for about 5 minutes until soft. Add the corn kernels and sauté 2 minutes longer.

2 Carefully tip the contents of the pan into a food processor or blender. Process until smooth, scraping down the sides of the blender and adding a little of the stock, if necessary.

White Bean Soup

*Use dried haricot or lima beans
for this velvety soup.*

INGREDIENTS

Serves 4

¾ cup dried white beans, soaked in cold
    water overnight
2 to 3 tablespoons oil
2 large onions, chopped
4 celery stalks, chopped
1 parsnip, chopped
1 quart chicken stock
salt and freshly ground black pepper
chopped fresh cilantro and paprika,
    to garnish

1 Drain the beans and boil
rapidly in fresh water for
10 minutes. Drain, cover with
more fresh water, and simmer for
1 to 2 hours until soft. Reserve the
liquid and discard any bean skins
on the surface.

2 Heat the oil in a heavy pan.
Add the onions, celery, and
parsnip and sauté for 3 minutes.

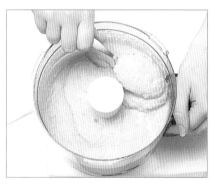

3 Add the cooked beans and
stock and continue cooking
until the vegetables are tender.
Leave the soup to cool slightly
and, using a food processor or
hand blender, blend the soup
until it is velvety smooth.

4 Reheat the soup slowly,
gradually adding some of the
bean liquid or a little water if it is
too thick. Season to taste.

5 To serve, transfer the soup
into warm bowls. Garnish
with fresh cilantro and paprika.

COOK'S TIP

You can, if you prefer, use a
14-ounce can cannellini or lima
beans instead of dried beans.
Drain and rinse them before
adding to the dish.

Pumpkin and Coconut Soup

Rich and sweet flavors are married beautifully with sharp and hot in this creamy Southeast Asian-influenced soup.

INGREDIENTS

Serves 4–6

2 garlic cloves, crushed

4 shallots, minced

½ teaspoon shrimp paste

1 tablespoon dried shrimp, soaked
   for 10 minutes and drained

1 lemongrass stalk, chopped

2 fresh green chilies, seeded

2½ cups chicken stock

1 pound pumpkin, cut into ¾-inch
   thick chunks

2½ cups coconut cream

2 tablespoons fish sauce

1 teaspoon sugar

4 ounces small cooked and shelled prawns

salt and freshly ground black pepper

to garnish:
   2 fresh red chilies, seeded and finely
      sliced
   10 to 12 fresh basil leaves

5 Add the shrimp and cook until they are heated through. Serve garnished with the sliced red chilies and basil leaves.

1 Using a mortar and pestle, grind the garlic, shallots, shrimp paste, dried shrimp, lemongrass, green chilies, and a pinch of salt into a paste.

2 In a large saucepan, bring the chicken stock to a boil. Add the paste and stir until it dissolves.

3 Lower the heat, add the pumpkin, and simmer for 10 to 15 minutes, or until the pumpkin is tender.

4 Stir in the coconut cream and bring back to a simmer. Add the fish sauce, sugar, and ground black pepper to taste.

COOK'S TIP

Shrimp paste is popular in Asian cooking and is used to give food a savory flavor.

Shrimp and Corn Bisque

Hot-pepper sauce adds a touch of spice to this mild, creamy soup.

INGREDIENTS

Serves 4

2 tablespoons olive oil

1 onion, finely minced

4 tablespoons butter or margarine

2 tablespoons all-purpose flour

3 cups fish stock

1 cup milk

1 cup shelled cooked small shrimp, deveined if necessary

1½ cups whole corn kernels

½ teaspoon chopped fresh dill or thyme

hot-pepper sauce

½ cup light cream

salt

sprigs of fresh dill, to garnish

1 Heat the olive oil in a large heavy-bottomed pan. Add the onion and cook over low heat for 8 to 10 minutes until soft.

2 Meanwhile, melt the butter or margarine in a medium-size saucepan. Add the flour and cook for 1 to 2 minutes, stirring. Stir in the stock and milk, bring to a boil, and cook for 5 to 8 minutes, stirring frequently.

3 Cut each shrimp into 2 or 3 pieces. Add to the onion with the corn kernels and dill or thyme and cook for 2 to 3 minutes. Remove from the heat.

4 Stir the sauce mixture into the shrimp and corn mixture. Remove 3 cups of the soup and purée in a blender or food processor. Return it to the rest of the soup in the pan and stir well. Season with salt and hot-pepper sauce to taste.

5 Add the cream and stir to blend. Heat the soup almost to boiling point, stirring frequently.

6 Ladle into warm soup bowls and serve hot, garnished with sprigs of dill.

Shrimp Bisque

The classic French method for making a bisque requires pushing the shellfish through a tamis, *or drum strainer. This recipe is simpler and the result is just as smooth.*

INGREDIENTS

Serves 6 to 8

1½ pounds small or medium cooked
    shrimp in their shells
1½ tablespoons vegetable oil
2 onions, halved and sliced
1 large carrot, sliced
2 celery stalks, sliced
2¼ quarts water
a few drops of lemon juice
2 tablespoons tomato paste
bouquet garni
4 tablespoons butter
⅓ cup all-purpose flour
3 to 4 tablespoons brandy
⅔ cup whipping cream

1 Remove the heads from the shrimp and peel away the shells: Reserve the heads and shells for the stock. Place the shelled shrimp in a covered bowl and chill in the refrigerator.

2 Heat the oil in a large saucepan. Add the heads and shells and cook over high heat, stirring, until they start to brown. Lower the heat to medium. Add the vegetables and fry slowly, stirring occasionally, for 5 minutes until the onions start to soften.

3 Add the water, lemon juice, tomato paste, and bouquet garni. Bring the stock to a boil. Lower the heat, cover, and simmer for 25 minutes. Strain the stock.

4 Melt the butter in a heavy-bottomed pan over medium heat. Stir in the flour and cook until just golden, stirring occasionally.

5 Add the brandy. Gradually pour in half the shrimp stock, whisking vigorously until smooth, then whisk in the remaining liquid. Season if necessary. Lower the heat, cover, and simmer for 5 minutes, stirring frequently.

6 Strain the soup into the rinsed saucepan. Add the cream and a little extra lemon juice to taste. Stir in most of the reserved shrimp and cook over medium heat, stirring frequently, until hot. Serve at once, garnished with the remaining shrimp.

COOK'S TIP

If you prefer, you can omit the brandy without taking away from the delicious flavor.

Fish and Sweet Potato Soup

The subtle sweetness of the potato, combined with the fish and the aromatic flavor of oregano, makes this an appetizing soup.

INGREDIENTS

Serves 4

½ onion, chopped

generous 1 cup peeled and diced
   sweet potato

6 ounces boneless white fish fillet, skinned

½ cup chopped carrot

1 teaspoon chopped fresh oregano, or
   ½ teaspoon dried oregano

½ teaspoon ground cinnamon

1½ quarts fish stock

5 tablespoons light cream

chopped fresh parsley, to garnish

1 Put the onion, sweet potato, white fish, carrot, oregano, cinnamon, and half of the fish stock in a saucepan. Bring to a boil. Lower the heat and simmer for 20 minutes, or until the potato is cooked.

2 Leave to cool, then pour into a blender or food processor and blend until smooth.

3 Return the soup to the rinsed pan. Add the remaining fish stock and slowly bring to a boil. Lower the heat to low and add the light cream. Heat through slowly without boiling, stirring occasionally.

4 Serve hot in warm soup bowls, garnished with the chopped fresh parsley.

VARIATION

Garnish with chopped fresh tarragon instead of parsley.

Squash Soup with Horseradish Cream

V

The combination of cream, curry powder, and horseradish makes a wonderful topping for this soup.

INGREDIENTS

Serves 6

1 butternut squash

1 cooking apple

2 tablespoons butter

1 onion, minced

1 to 2 teaspoons curry powder, plus extra
   to garnish

3¾ cups vegetable stock

1 teaspoon chopped fresh sage

⅔ cup apple juice

salt and freshly ground black pepper

lime shreds, to garnish (optional)

For the horseradish cream

4 tablespoons heavy cream

2 teaspoons horseradish sauce

/2 teaspoon curry powder

1 Peel the squash, remove the seeds, and chop the flesh. Peel, core, and chop the apple.

2 Melt the butter in a large saucepan. Add the onion and cook, stirring occasionally, for 5 minutes until soft. Stir in the curry powder and cook to bring out the flavor, stirring constantly, for 2 minutes.

3 Add the stock, squash, apple, and sage. Bring to a boil. Lower the heat, cover and simmer for 20 minutes until the squash and apple are soft.

4 Meanwhile, make the horseradish cream. Whip the cream in a bowl until stiff. Stir in the horseradish sauce and curry powder. Chill until required.

5 Purée the soup in a blender or food processor. Return to the rinsed pan and add the apple juice, with salt and pepper to taste. Reheat slowly, without boiling.

6 Serve the soup in warm bowls, topped with a spoonful of horseradish cream and a dusting of curry powder. Garnish with a few lime shreds, if you like.

Thai-Style Chicken Soup

A fragrant blend of coconut milk, lemongrass, ginger, and lime makes a delicious soup, with just a hint of warming chili.

INGREDIENTS

Serves 4

1 teaspoon oil

1–2 fresh red chilies, seeded and chopped

2 garlic cloves, crushed

1 large leek, finely sliced

2½ cups chicken stock

1¾ cups coconut milk

1 pound skinless, boneless chicken thighs, cut into bite-size pieces

2 tablespoons Thai fish sauce

1 lemongrass stalk, split

1-inch piece fresh ginger root, peeled and minced

1 teaspoon sugar

4 kaffir lime leaves (optional)

¾ cup frozen peas, thawed

3 tablespoons chopped fresh cilantro

1 Heat the oil in a large saucepan. Add the chilies and garlic and cook for about 2 minutes. Add the leek and cook for 2 minutes longer.

2 Stir in the stock and coconut milk and bring to a boil over medium-high heat.

3 Add the chicken, fish sauce, lemongrass, ginger, sugar, and lime leaves, if using. Lower the heat and simmer, covered, for 15 minutes until the chicken is tender, stirring occasionally.

4 Add the peas and cook for 3 minutes longer. Remove the lemongrass and stir in the cilantro just before serving.

Spicy Chicken and Mushroom Soup

This creamy chicken soup makes a hearty meal. Serve it piping hot with fresh garlic bread.

INGREDIENTS

Serves 4

6 tablespoons unsalted butter

½ teaspoon crushed garlic

1 teaspoon garam masala

1 teaspoon crushed black peppercorns

1 teaspoon salt

¼ teaspoon freshly grated nutmeg

8 ounces chicken, skinned and boned

1 medium leek, sliced

generous 1 cup sliced mushrooms

⅓ cup whole corn kernels

1¼ cups water

1 cup light cream

1 tablespoon chopped fresh cilantro

1 teaspoon crushed dried red chilies, to garnish (optional)

1 Melt the butter in a medium saucepan. Lower the heat slightly and add the garlic and garam masala. Lower the heat even more and add the black peppercorns, salt, and nutmeg.

2 Cut the chicken pieces into very fine strips and add to the pan with the leek, mushrooms, and corn kernel. Cook for 5 to 7 minutes until the chicken is cooked through, stirring constantly.

3 Remove from the heat and leave to cool slightly. Transfer three-quarters of the mixture into a food processor or blender. Add the water and process for about 1 minute.

4 Pour the resulting purée back into the saucepan with the rest of the mixture and bring to a boil over medium heat. Lower the heat and stir in the cream.

5 Add the fresh cilantro. Taste and adjust the seasoning. Serve hot, garnished with crushed red chilies, if liked.

Chicken and Almond Soup

This spicy soup makes an excellent lunch or supper dish when served with Indian naan bread.

INGREDIENTS

Serves 4

6 tablespoons unsalted butter

1 leek, chopped

½ teaspoon shredded fresh ginger root

¾ cup blanched almonds, very finely ground

1 teaspoon salt

½ teaspoon crushed black peppercorns

1 fresh green chilli, chopped

1 carrot, sliced

½ cup frozen peas

1 cup skinned, boned, and cubed chicken

2 tablespoons chopped fresh cilantro

2 cups water

1 cup light cream

4 sprigs of fresh cilantro

1 Melt the unsalted butter in a deep skillet or wok. Add the chopped leek and the ginger root and sauté until soft but only just turning brown.

2 Lower the heat and add the ground almonds, salt, peppercorns, chili, carrot, peas and chicken. Fry for about 10 minutes, or until the chicken is cooked through and tender, stirring constantly. Add the cilantro.

3 Remove from the heat and leave to cool slightly. Transfer the mixture to a food processor or blender and process for about 1½ minutes. Pour in the water and blend for 30 seconds longer.

4 Pour back into the rinsed pan and bring to a boil, stirring occasionally. Once it has boiled, lower the heat and gradually stir in the cream. Simmer for 2 minutes longer, stirring from time to time. Serve garnished with the sprigs of fresh cilantro.

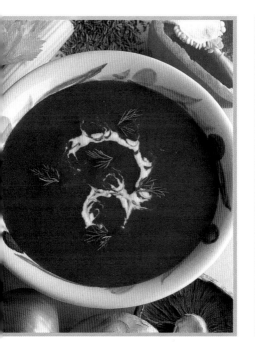

WARMING
WINTER SOUPS

Borscht

V

A simply stunning color, this classic Russian soup is the perfect dish to serve when you want to offer something a little different.

INGREDIENTS

Serves 6

1 onion, chopped

3 cups peeled and chopped beets

2 celery stalks, chopped

$\frac{1}{2}$ red bell pepper, chopped

$1\frac{1}{2}$ cups chopped mushrooms

1 large cooking apple, chopped

2 tablespoons butter

2 tablespoons sunflower oil

$2\frac{1}{4}$ quarts stock or water

1 teaspoon cumin seeds

a pinch of dried thyme

1 large bay leaf

fresh lemon juice

salt and freshly ground black pepper

For the garnish

$\frac{2}{3}$ cup sour cream

a few sprigs of fresh dill

COOK'S TIP

The flavor of this marvelous soup matures and improves if it is made the day before it is needed.

1 Place the chopped vegetables and apple in a large saucepan with the butter, oil, and 3 tablespoons of the stock or water. Cover and cook slowly for about 15 minutes, shaking the pan occasionally.

2 Stir in the cumin seeds and cook for 1 minute. Add the remaining stock or water, the thyme, bay leaf, lemon juice, and seasoning to taste.

3 Bring the soup to a boil. Cover the pan and turn down the heat to a slow simmer. Cook for about 30 minutes.

4 Strain the vegetables and reserve the liquid. Process the vegetables in a food processor or blender until they are smooth and creamy.

5 Return the vegetables to the rinsed pan. Add the reserved stock and reheat. Check the seasoning.

6 Divide into soup bowls. Garnish with swirls of sour cream in each bowl and top with a few sprigs of fresh dill.

Curried Celery Soup

An unusual but stimulating combination of flavors, this warming soup is an excellent way to transform celery. Serve with warm whole wheat rolls.

INGREDIENTS

Serves 4 to 6

2 teaspoons olive oil

1 onion, chopped

1 leek, sliced

5½ cups chopped celery

1 tablespoon medium or hot
    curry powder

1½ cups washed and diced unpeeled
    potatoes

3¾ cups vegetable stock

1 bouquet garni

2 tablespoons chopped fresh mixed herbs

salt

celery seeds and leaves, to garnish

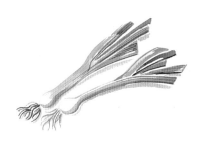

1 Heat the oil in a large saucepan. Add the onion, leek, and celery, cover, and cook slowly for about 10 minutes, stirring occasionally.

2 Add the curry powder and continue cooking for 2 minutes, stirring occasionally.

3 Add the potatoes, stock, and bouquet garni, cover, and bring to a boil. Simmer for about 20 minutes until the vegetables are tender, but not too soft.

4 Remove and discard the bouquet garni. Set aside the soup to cool slightly before it is processed.

5 Transfer the soup to a blender or food processor and process in batches until smooth.

6 Add the mixed herbs, season to taste with salt and process briefly again. Return to the saucepan and reheat slowly until piping hot. Ladle into warm bowls and garnish each one with a sprinkling of celery seeds and a few celery leaves before serving.

VARIATION

For a change, use celery root and sweet potatoes in place of celery and standard potatoes.

Nettle Soup

A country-style soup which is a tasty variation of the classic Irish potato soup. Use wild nettles if you can find them, or a washed head of round lettuce if you prefer.

INGREDIENTS

Serves 4

½ cup butter

3 cups sliced onions

3 cups potatoes, cut into chunks

3 cups chicken stock

1 ounce nettle leaves

a small bunch of chives, snipped

salt and freshly ground black pepper

heavy cream, to serve

2 Wearing latex gloves, remove the nettle leaves from their stems. Rinse the leaves under cold running water, then dry on paper towels. Add to the saucepan and cook for 5 minutes longer.

3 Ladle the soup into a blender or food processor and process until smooth. Return to a clean saucepan and season well. Stir in the chives and serve with a swirl of cream and a sprinkling of pepper.

1 Melt the butter in a large saucepan. Add the sliced onions, cover, and cook for about 5 minutes until just soft. Add the potatoes to the saucepan with the chicken stock, cover, and cook for 25 minutes longer.

COOK'S TIP

If you prefer, cut the vegetables finely and leave the soup chunky rather than puréeing it.

Leek, Parsnip, and Ginger Soup

V

A flavorsome winter warmer, with the added spiciness of fresh ginger.

Serves 4 to 6

2 tablespoons olive oil

2 cups sliced leeks

2 tablespoons peeled and minced
   ginger root

5 cups roughly chopped parsnips

1¼ cups dry white wine

5 cups vegetable stock or water

salt and freshly ground black pepper

fromage blanc and paprika, to garnish

1 Heat the oil in a large pan. Add the leeks and ginger and cook slowly for 2 to 3 minutes until the leeks start to become soft.

2 Add the parsnips and cook for 7 to 8 minutes longer until they begin to become soft.

3 Pour in the wine and stock or water and bring to a boil. Lower the heat and simmer for 20 to 30 minutes, or until the parsnips are tender.

4 Purée in a blender or food processor until smooth. Season to taste. Reheat and garnish with a swirl of fromage blanc and a light dusting of paprika.

Green Pea Soup with Spinach

This lovely green soup was invented by the wife of a seventeenth-century British member of parliament, and it has stood the test of time.

INGREDIENTS

Serves 6

generous 3 cups shelled fresh or
    frozen peas
1 leek, finely sliced
2 garlic cloves, crushed
2 bacon slices, finely diced
1¼ quarts ham or chicken stock
2 tablespoons olive oil
1 cup shredded fresh spinach
⅓ cup finely shredded white cabbage
½ small lettuce, finely shredded
1 celery stalk, minced
a large handful of parsley, minced
½ carton cress
4 teaspoons chopped fresh mint
a pinch of ground mace
salt and freshly ground black pepper

1 Put the peas, leek, garlic, and bacon in a large saucepan. Add the stock and bring to a boil. Lower the heat and simmer for 20 minutes.

2 About 5 minutes before the pea mixture is ready, heat the oil in another large saucepan.

3 Add the spinach, cabbage, lettuce, celery and herbs to the skillet. Cover and sweat over low heat until soft.

4 Transfer the pea mixture to a blender or food processor and process until smooth. Add to the sweated vegetables and herbs and heat through. Season with mace, salt and pepper and serve.

Spicy Carrot Soup with Garlic Croutons

V

Carrot soup is given a touch of spice with coriander, cumin and cayenne pepper.

INGREDIENTS

Serves 6

1 tablespoon olive oil

1 large onion, chopped

3¾ cups sliced carrots

1 teaspoon each ground coriander, ground cumin, and cayenne pepper

3¾ cups vegetable stock

salt and freshly ground black pepper

sprigs of fresh cilantro, to garnish

For the garlic croutons

a little olive oil

2 garlic cloves, crushed

4 slices bread, crusts removed, cut into ½-inch cubes

1 To make the soup, heat the oil in a large saucepan. Add the onion and carrots and cook slowly for 5 minutes, stirring occasionally. Add the ground spices and cook for 1 minute longer, stirring.

2 Stir in the stock and bring to a boil. Cover and simmer for about 45 minutes until the carrots are tender.

3 Meanwhile, make the garlic croutons. Heat the oil in a skillet. Add the garlic and cook slowly for 30 seconds, stirring. Add the bread cubes, turn them over in the oil and fry over medium heat for a few minutes until crisp and golden brown all over, turning frequently. Drain on paper towels and keep warm.

4 Purée the soup in a blender or food processor until smooth. Season to taste with salt and pepper. Return the soup to the rinsed saucepan and reheat slowly. Serve hot, sprinkled with garlic croutons and garnished with cilantro sprigs.

Curried Carrot and Apple Soup

The combination of carrot, curry powder, and apple is a highly successful one. Curried fruit is delicious.

INGREDIENTS

Serves 4

2 teaspoons sunflower oil

1 tablespoon mild korma curry powder

3½ cups chopped carrots

1 large onion, chopped

1 tart cooking apple, chopped

3 cups chicken stock

salt and freshly ground black pepper

plain yogurt and carrot curls, to garnish

1 Heat the oil in a large, heavy-bottomed pan. Add the curry powder and fry for 2 to 3 minutes.

2 Add the carrots, onion, and cooking apple and stir well until coated with the curry powder. Cover the pan.

3 Cook over low heat for about 15 minutes, shaking the pan occasionally, until soft. Spoon the vegetable mixture into a food processor or blender, then add half the stock and process until the mixture is smooth.

4 Return to the pan and pour in the remaining stock. Bring the soup to a boil and adjust the seasoning before serving in bowls, garnished with a swirl of yogurt and a few curls of raw carrot.

Pumpkin Soup

V

The sweet flavor of pumpkin is excellent in soups, teaming well with other savory ingredients, such as onions and potatoes, to make warm and comforting dishes. For added flavor in this recipe, roast the pumpkin chunks before adding them to the soup.

INGREDIENTS

Serves 4–6

1 tablespoon sunflower oil

2 tablespoons butter

1 large onion, sliced

6 cups pumpkin cut into large chunks

3 cups sliced potatoes

2½ cups vegetable stock

a good pinch of freshly grated nutmeg

1 teaspoon chopped fresh tarragon

2½ cups milk

1 to 2 teaspoons lemon juice

salt and freshly ground black pepper

1 Heat the oil and butter in a heavy-bottomed saucepan. Add the onion and fry for 4 to 5 minutes over low heat until soft but not brown, stirring frequently.

2 Add the pumpkin and potatoes and stir well. Cover and sweat over low heat for about 10 minutes until the vegetables are almost tender, stirring occasionally to stop them sticking.

3 Stir in the stock, nutmeg, tarragon, and seasoning. Bring to a boil. Lower the heat and simmer for about 10 minutes until the vegetables are completely tender.

4 Leave the soup to cool slightly. Pour into a food processor or blender and process until smooth. Pour back into the rinsed saucepan and add the milk. Heat slowly and taste, adding the lemon juice and extra seasoning, if necessary. Serve piping hot.

Sweet Potato and Red Pepper Soup

As colorful as it is good to eat, this soup is a certain winner.

INGREDIENTS

Serves 6

2 red bell peppers (about 8 ounces), seeded and cubed

generous 4 cups diced sweet potatoes

1 onion, roughly chopped

2 large garlic cloves, roughly chopped

1¼ cups dry white wine

1¼ quarts vegetable stock

hot-pepper sauce, to taste

salt and freshly ground black pepper

fresh chunky bread, to serve

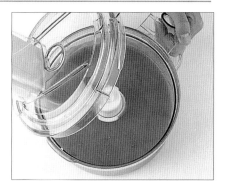

1 Dice a small quantity of the red pepper for the garnish; set aside. Put the rest into a saucepan with the sweet potatoes, onion, garlic, wine, and vegetable stock and bring to a boil. Lower the heat and simmer for 30 minutes, or until all the vegetables are soft.

2 Transfer the soup to a blender or food processor and process until smooth. Season to taste with salt, pepper, and a generous dash of hot-pepper sauce. Cool slightly. Garnish with the reserved diced red pepper and serve warm or at room temperature.

Sweet Potato and Parsnip Soup

V

The sweetness of the two root vegetables comes through strongly in this delicious soup.

INGREDIENTS

Serves 6

1 tablespoon sunflower oil

1 large leek, sliced

2 celery stalks, chopped

4 cups diced sweet potatoes

1½ cups diced parsnips

3¾ cups vegetable stock

salt and freshly ground black pepper

For the garnish

1 tablespoon chopped fresh parsley

roasted strips of sweet potatoes and
  parsnips

1 Heat the oil in a large saucepan. Add the leek, celery, sweet potatoes, and parsnips and cook slowly for about 5 minutes, stirring to prevent them browning or sticking to the pan.

2 Stir in the vegetable stock and bring to a boil. Lower the heat, cover and simmer for about 25 minutes, or until the vegetables are tender, stirring occasionally. Season to taste. Remove the pan from the heat and let the soup cool slightly.

3 Purée the soup in a blender or food processor until smooth.

Return the soup to the rinsed pan and reheat slowly. Ladle into warm soup bowls to serve and sprinkle with the chopped parsley and roasted strips of sweet potatoes and parsnips.

V

Root Vegetable Soup

Simmer a selection of your favorite root vegetables together for this warming and satisfying soup. Its creaminess comes from adding crème fraîche or sour cream just before serving.

INGREDIENTS

Serves 6

3 carrots, chopped

1 large potato, chopped

1 large parsnip, chopped

1 large turnip or small rutabaga, chopped

1 onion, chopped

2 tablespoons sunflower oil

2 tablespoons butter

1½ quarts cups water

1 piece fresh ginger root, peeled and
    grated

1¼ cups milk

3 tablespoons crème fraîche or sour cream

2 tablespoons chopped fresh dill

1 tablespoon lemon juice

salt and freshly ground black pepper

sprigs of fresh dill, to garnish

1 Put the carrots, potato, parsnip, turnip or rutabaga, and onion into a large saucepan with the oil and butter and fry lightly. Cover and sweat the vegetables over low heat for 15 minutes, shaking the pan occasionally.

2 Pour in the water, bring to a boil, and season well. Cover and simmer for 20 minutes until the vegetables are soft.

3 Strain the vegetables, reserving the stock. Add the ginger and vegetables to a food processor or blender and purée until smooth. Return the puréed mixture and stock to the pan. Add the milk and stir while the soup gently reheats.

4 Remove from the heat and stir in the crème fraîche or sour cream, plus the dill and lemon juice. Season if necessary. Reheat the soup: Do not let it boil, or it may curdle. Serve garnished with sprigs of dill.

Leek and Thyme Soup

This is a filling, heart-warming soup, which can be blended to a smooth purée or served as it is here, in its original peasant style.

INGREDIENTS

Serves 4

2 pounds leeks

1 pound potatoes

¹⁄₂ cup butter

1 large sprig of fresh thyme, plus extra to garnish (optional)

1¹⁄₄ cups milk

salt and freshly ground black pepper

4 tablespoons heavy cream, to serve

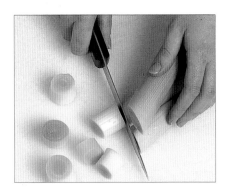

1 Top and tail the leeks. If you are using big winter leeks, strip away all the coarse outer leaves, then cut the leeks into thick slices. Rinse thoroughly under cold water.

2 Cut the potatoes into rough dice, about 1 inch, and dry on paper towels.

3 Melt the butter in a large saucepan. Add the leeks and 1 sprig of thyme, cover and cook for 4 to 5 minutes until soft. Add the potato pieces and just enough cold water to cover the vegetables. Re-cover and cook over low heat for 30 minutes.

4 Pour in the milk and season with salt and pepper. Cover and simmer for 30 minutes longer. You will find that some of the potato breaks up, leaving you with a semi-puréed and lumpy soup.

5 Remove the sprig of thyme: The leaves will have fallen into the soup. Serve, adding 1 tablespoon cream and a garnish of thyme to each portion, if using.

Mushroom and Herb Potage

Do not worry if this soup is not completely smooth—it is especially nice when it has a slightly nutty, textured consistency.

INGREDIENTS

Serves 4

2 ounces smoked bacon

1 onion, chopped

1 tablespoon sunflower oil

12 ounces open portobello mushrooms or a mixture of wild and cremini mushrooms

2½ cups good meat stock

2 tablespoons sweet sherry

2 tablespoons chopped fresh mixed herbs, such as sage, rosemary, thyme, and marjoram, or 2 teaspoons Italian seasoning

salt and freshly ground black pepper

a few sprigs of sage or marjoram, to garnish

4 tablespoons thick plain yogurt or sour cream, to serve

2 Add the onion and soften, adding oil if necessary. Wipe the mushrooms clean, roughly chop, and add to the pan. Cover and sweat until they are completely soft and their liquid has run out.

1 Roughly chop the bacon and place in a large saucepan. Cook slowly until all the fat comes out of the bacon.

3 Add the stock, sherry, herbs or Italian seasoning, and salt and black pepper to taste. Cover and simmer for 10 to 12 minutes. Process the soup in a food processor or blender until smooth, but don't worry if you still have a slightly textured result.

4 Check the seasoning and heat through. Serve with a dollop of yogurt or sour cream and a sprig of fresh sage or marjoram in each bowl.

Mushroom, Celery, and Garlic Soup

This robust soup with the dominant flavor of mushrooms is enhanced with garlic, while celery introduces a contrasting note.

INGREDIENTS

Serves 4

4½ cups chopped mushrooms

4 celery stalks, chopped

3 garlic cloves

3 tablespoons dry sherry or white wine

3 cups chicken stock

2 tablespoons Worcestershire sauce

1 teaspoon freshly grated nutmeg

salt and freshly ground black pepper

celery leaves, to garnish

1 Place the mushrooms, celery, and garlic in a pan and stir in the sherry or wine. Cover and cook over low heat for 30 to 40 minutes until the vegetables are tender.

2 Add half the stock and purée in a food processor or blender until smooth. Return to the pan and add the remaining stock, the Worcestershire sauce, and nutmeg.

3 Bring to a boil and season to taste with salt and pepper. Serve hot, garnished with celery leaves.

Mushroom and Bread Soup with Parsley

Thickened with bread, this rich mushroom soup will warm you up on cold winter days. It makes a terrific hearty lunch.

INGREDIENTS

Serves 8

6 tablespoons unsalted butter

2 pounds portobello mushrooms, sliced

2 onions, roughly chopped

2½ cups milk

8 slices white bread

4 tablespoons chopped fresh parsley

1¼ cups heavy cream

salt and freshly ground black pepper

1 Melt the butter. Add the sliced mushrooms and onions and sauté for about 10 minutes until soft but not brown. Stir in the milk.

2 Tear the bread into pieces, drop them into the soup, and leave them to soak for 15 minutes. Purée the soup and return it to the pan. Add 3 tablespoons of the parsley, the cream, and seasoning. Reheat, without boiling. Serve garnished with the remaining parsley.

French Onion Soup

In France, this standard bistro fare is served so frequently it is simply referred to as gratinée.

INGREDIENTS

Serves 6 to 8

1 tablespoon butter

2 tablespoons olive oil

4 large onions, finely sliced

2 to 5 garlic cloves

1 teaspoon sugar

½ teaspoon dried thyme

2 tablespoons all-purpose flour

½ cup dry white wine

2¼ quarts beef stock

2 tablespoons brandy (optional)

6 to 8 thick slices French bread, toasted

3 cups grated Gruyère or Swiss cheese

1 In a large, heavy-bottomed saucepan or flameproof casserole, heat the butter and oil over medium-high heat. Add the onions and cook for 10 to 12 minutes until they are soft and beginning to brown.

2 Putting one garlic clove aside, finely chop the rest and add to the onions. Add the sugar and thyme and continue cooking over medium heat for 30 to 35 minutes until the onions are brown, stirring frequently.

3 Sprinkle the flour over and stir until well blended. Stir in the wine and stock and bring to a boil. Skim off any foam from the surface. Lower the heat and simmer for 45 minutes. Stir in the brandy, if using.

4 Heat the broiler. Rub each slice of toasted French bread with the remaining garlic clove. Place 6 or 8 flameproof soup bowls on a cookie sheet and fill them about three-quarters full with the onion soup.

5 Float a piece of toast in each bowl. Top with grated cheese, dividing it evenly. Broil about 6 inches from the heat for 3 to 4 minutes until the cheese begins to melt and bubble. Serve piping hot.

Spanish Garlic Soup

This is a simple and traditional soup, made with garlic, which is one of the most popular ingredients in the quick cook's kitchen.

INGREDIENTS

Serves 4

2 tablespoons olive oil

4 large garlic cloves, peeled

4 slices French bread, about ¼ inch thick

1 tablespoon paprika

1 quart beef stock

¼ teaspoon ground cumin

a pinch of saffron strands

4 eggs

salt and freshly ground black pepper

chopped fresh parsley, to garnish

1 Heat the oven to 450°F. Heat the oil in a large pan. Add the whole garlic cloves and cook until golden; remove and set aside. Fry the bread in the oil until it turns a golden brown; set aside.

2 Add the paprika to the pan and fry for a few seconds. Stir in the beef stock, cumin, and saffron. Add the reserved garlic, crushing the cloves with the back of a wooden spoon, and season with salt and pepper. Cook for about 5 minutes.

3 Ladle the soup into 4 ovenproof bowls and break 1 egg into each one. Place a slice of fried bread on top of each egg. Put the bowls in the oven for 3 to 4 minutes until the eggs are set. Sprinkle each portion with parsley and serve at once.

COOK'S TIP

When you turn on the oven, put a cookie sheet in at the same time. Stand the soup bowls on the hot cookie sheet when you put them in the oven and you will be able to remove them easily when the eggs are set.

Onion and Pancetta Soup

This warming winter soup comes from Umbria, where it is sometimes thickened with beaten eggs and plenty of grated Parmesan cheese. It is then served on top of a piece of hot toast–like savory scrambled eggs.

INGREDIENTS

Serves 4

4 ounces pancetta slices, rinds removed, roughly chopped

2 tablespoons olive oil

1 tablespoon butter

5½ cups finely sliced onions

2 teaspoons sugar

about 1¼ quarts chicken stock

2½ cups peeled and roughly chopped Italian plum tomatoes

a few fresh basil leaves, shredded

salt and freshly ground black pepper

grated Parmesan cheese, to serve

1 Put the chopped pancetta in a large saucepan and heat slowly, stirring constantly, until the fat runs. Increase the heat to medium. Add the oil, butter, onions, and sugar and stir well to mix.

2 Half-cover the pan and cook the onions slowly for about 20 minutes until golden: Stir frequently and lower the heat if necessary.

3 Add the stock, tomatoes, and salt and pepper and bring to a boil, stirring. Lower the heat, half-cover the pan, and simmer, stirring occasionally, for about 30 minutes.

4 Check the consistency of the soup and add a little more stock or water if it is too thick.

5 Just before serving, stir in most of the basil and adjust the seasoning to taste. Serve hot, garnished with the remaining shredded basil. Hand around the freshly grated Parmesan separately for sprinkling over each portion.

COOK'S TIP

Look for Vidalia onions, from Vidalia, Georgia, to make this soup. They have a sweet flavor and attractive, pale yellow flesh.

V

Spicy Tomato and Cilantro Soup

Heartwarming soup is always a favorite. Deliciously spicy, it is also the perfect soup to prepare for a cold winter's day.

INGREDIENTS

Serves 4

1½ pounds tomatoes

2 tablespoons vegetable oil

1 bay leaf

4 scallions, chopped

1 teaspoon salt

½ teaspoon crushed garlic

1 teaspoon crushed black peppercorns

2 tablespoons chopped fresh cilantro

3 cups water

1 tablespoon cornstarch

2 tablespoons light cream, to serve

COOK'S TIP

If the only fresh tomatoes available are pale and underripe, add 1 tablespoon tomato paste to the pan with the chopped tomatoes. This will enhance the color and flavor of the soup.

1 To peel the tomatoes, plunge them into very hot water. Using a slotted spoon, lift them out almost at once. The skin should peel off quickly and easily. Once this is done, chop the tomatoes roughly.

2 In a medium-size saucepan, heat the oil. Add the tomatoes, bay leaf, and scallions and fry for a few minutes until soft and translucent, but not brown.

3 Add the salt, crushed garlic, peppercorns, and fresh cilantro to the tomato mixture. Stir in the water.

4 Bring to mixture to a boil. Lower the heat and simmer for 15 to 20 minutes. Meanwhile, dissolve the cornstarch in a little cold water; set aside.

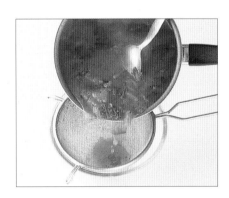

5 Remove the soup from the heat and press through a strainer placed over a bowl. Discard the strained vegetables.

6 Return the soup to the pan. Add the cornstarch mixture and stir over low heat for about 3 minutes until thick.

7 Pour into individual soup bowls and serve piping hot, with a swirl of cream.

Tomato and Vermicelli Soup

The vermicelli is lightly fried before being simmered in this tasty soup.

INGREDIENTS

Serves 4

2 tablespoons olive or corn oil

⅓ cup vermicelli

1 onion, roughly chopped

1 garlic clove, chopped

3 cups peeled, seeded, and roughly chopped tomatoes

1 quart chicken stock

¼ teaspoon sugar

1 tablespoon finely chopped fresh cilantro, plus extra to garnish

salt and freshly ground black pepper

⅓ cup grated Parmesan cheese, to serve

1 Heat the oil in a skillet. Add the vermicelli and sauté over medium heat until golden brown: Do not let the strands burn.

2 Remove the pan from the heat. Lift out the vermicelli with a draining spoon and drain on paper towels; set aside.

3 Purée the onion, garlic, and tomatoes in a food processor until smooth. Return the skillet to the heat. When the oil is hot, add the purée. Cook, stirring constantly, for about 5 minutes, or until thick.

4 Transfer the purée to a saucepan. Add the vermicelli and pour in the stock. Season with sugar, salt, and pepper. Stir in the cilantro and bring to a boil. Lower the heat, cover the pan, and simmer the soup until the vermicelli is tender.

5 Serve in hot bowls, sprinkled with fresh cilantro. Offer the Parmesan cheese separately.

Lightly Spiced Tomato Soup

Simple and quick to make, this tomato soup will soon become one of your firm favorites.

INGREDIENTS

Serves 4

1 tablespoon corn or peanut oil

1 onion, finely chopped

6 cups peeled, seeded, and chopped tomatoes

2 cups chicken stock

2 large sprigs of fresh cilantro

salt and freshly ground black pepper

coarsely ground black pepper, to serve

1 Heat the oil in a large saucepan. Add the onion and slowly fry, stirring frequently, for about 5 minutes until it is soft and transparent, but not brown.

2 Add the chopped tomatoes, chicken stock, and cilantro to the pan and bring to a boil. Lower the heat, cover the pan, and simmer for 15 minutes, or until the tomatoes are soft.

3 Remove and discard the cilantro. Press the soup through a strainer and return it to the rinsed pan. Season and heat through. Serve sprinkled with coarsely ground black pepper.

Broccoli and Bread Soup

Broccoli grows abundantly around Rome and is served in this traditional Italian soup with garlic toasts.

INGREDIENTS

Serves 6

1½ pounds broccoli spears

1¾ quarts chicken or vegetable stock

1 tablespoon lemon juice

salt and freshly ground black pepper

To serve

6 slices white bread

1 large garlic clove, cut in half

grated Parmesan cheese (optional)

1 Using a small, sharp knife, peel the broccoli stems, starting from the base and pulling gently up toward the flowerets: The peel should come off easily. Chop the broccoli into small chunks.

2 Bring the stock to a boil in a large saucepan. Add the broccoli and simmer for about 10 minutes until soft.

3 Purée about half of the soup and stir into the rest of the soup. Season with salt, pepper, and lemon juice.

4 Reheat the soup. Toast the bread, rub with garlic, and cut into quarters. Place 3 or 4 pieces of toast in the bottom of each soup bowl. Ladle the soup over. Serve at once, with Parmesan if liked.

Tomato and Bread Soup

This colorful Florentine recipe was created to use up stale bread. It can be made with very ripe fresh or canned plum tomatoes.

INGREDIENTS

Serves 4

6 tablespoons olive oil

small piece dried chili, crumbled
    (optional)

1½ cups stale bread, cut into
    1-inch cubes

1 onion, minced

2 garlic cloves, minced

5½ cups peeled and chopped ripe
    tomatoes, or 2 x 14-ounce cans
    peeled plum tomatoes, chopped

3 tablespoons chopped fresh basil

1½ quarts light meat stock or water, or a
    combination of both

salt and freshly ground black pepper

extra-virgin olive oil, to serve (optional)

1 Heat 4 tablespoons of the oil in a large saucepan. Add the chili, if using, and stir for 1 to 2 minutes. Add the bread cubes and cook until golden. Transfer to a plate and drain on paper towels.

2 Add the remaining oil, the onion, and garlic to the pan and cook until the onion is soft. Stir in the tomatoes, basil, and the reserved bread cubes. Season with salt. Cook over medium heat, stirring occasionally, for about 15 minutes.

3 Meanwhile, heat the stock or water to simmering. Add it to the tomato mixture and stir well. Bring to a boil. Lower the heat slightly and simmer for 20 minutes.

4 Remove the soup from the heat. Use a fork to mash together the tomatoes and bread. Season with pepper, and more salt if necessary. Leave to stand for 10 minutes. Just before serving, swirl in a little extra-virgin olive oil, if liked.

Garlicky Lentil Soup

High in fiber, lentils make a flavor-packed soup. Unlike most legumes, they do not need to be soaked before being cooked.

INGREDIENTS

Serves 6

1⅓ cups red lentils, rinsed and drained

2 onions, minced

2 large garlic cloves, minced

1 carrot, minced

2 tablespoons olive oil

2 bay leaves

a generous pinch of dried marjoram or
    oregano

1½ cups vegetable stock

2 tablespoons red-wine vinegar

salt and freshly ground black pepper

celery leaves, to garnish

crusty bread rolls, to serve

1 Put all the ingredients, except for the vinegar, seasoning, and garnish, in a large, heavy-bottomed saucepan. Bring to a boil over medium heat. Lower the heat and simmer for 1½ hours, stirring the soup occasionally to prevent the lentils from sticking to the bottom of the pan.

2 Remove the bay leaves and add the red-wine vinegar, with salt and pepper to taste. If the soup is too thick, thin it with a little extra vegetable stock or water. Serve the soup in hot bowls, garnished with celery leaves. Serve with warm crusty rolls.

COOK'S TIP

If you buy your lentils loose, remember to tip them into a strainer or colander and pick them over, removing any pieces of grit, before rinsing them.

Spiced Lentil Soup

A subtle blend of spices takes this warming soup to new heights. Serve it with crusty bread for a filling and satisfying lunch.

INGREDIENTS

Serves 6

2 onions, minced

2 garlic cloves, crushed

4 tomatoes, roughly chopped

½ teaspoon turmeric

1 teaspoon ground cumin

6 cardamom pods

½ cinnamon stick

1⅓ cups red lentils, rinsed and drained

3¾ cups water

14-ounce can coconut milk

1 tablespoon lime juice

salt and freshly ground black pepper

cumin seeds, to garnish

1 Put the onions, garlic, tomatoes, turmeric, cumin, cardamom pods, cinnamon, lentils, and water into a saucepan and bring to a boil. Lower the heat, cover, and simmer for 20 minutes, or until the lentils are soft.

2 Remove the cardamom pods and cinnamon stick. Purée the mixture in a blender or food processor. Press the soup through a strainer into the rinsed pan.

3 Reserve a little of the coconut milk for the garnish and add the remainder to the pan with the lime juice. Stir well and season with salt and pepper. Reheat the soup slowly without boiling. Swirl in the reserved coconut milk and garnish with cumin seeds. Serve piping hot.

South Indian Pepper Water

V

This is a highly soothing broth for cold winter evenings. Serve with the whole spices or strain and reheat, as you like. The lemon juice may be adjusted to taste, but this dish should be distinctly sour.

INGREDIENTS

Serves 2 to 4

2 tablespoons vegetable oil

½ teaspoon freshly ground black pepper

1 teaspoon cumin seeds

½ teaspoon mustard seeds

¼ teaspoon asafetida powder

2 whole dried red chilies

4 to 6 curry leaves

½ teaspoon turmeric

2 garlic cloves, crushed

1¼ cups tomato juice

juice of 2 lemons

½ cup water

salt

fresh cilantro leaves, chopped, to garnish

1 In a large skillet, heat the vegetable oil. Add the spices and garlic and fry until the chilies are almost black and the garlic is a golden brown.

2 Lower the heat and add the tomato juice, lemon juice, water, and salt to taste. Bring to a boil. Simmer for 10 minutes. Garnish with chopped cilantro and serve piping hot.

COOK'S TIP

Asafetida is a pungent powder used to enhance Indian vegetarian cooking. In its raw state it can smell very unpleasant, but this smell soon disappears once it is cooked.

Spicy Peanut Soup

A thick and warming vegetable soup, flavored with cayenne pepper and peanuts.

INGREDIENTS

Serves 6

2 tablespoons oil

1 large onion, minced

2 garlic cloves, crushed

1 teaspoon mild ground cayenne pepper

2 red bell peppers, seeded and minced

1½ cups minced carrots

1½ cups finely chopped potatoes

3 celery stalks, sliced

3¾ cups vegetable stock

6 tablespoons crunchy peanut butter

⅔ cup whole corn kernels

salt and freshly ground black pepper

roughly chopped unsalted roasted
   peanuts, to garnish

1 Heat the oil in a large pan. Add the onion and garlic and cook for about 3 minutes. Add the cayenne pepper and cook for 1 minute longer.

2 Add the red peppers, carrots, potatoes, and celery. Stir well and cook for 4 minutes longer, stirring occasionally.

3 Add the vegetable stock, peanut butter, and corn kernels, stirring until thoroughly combined.

4 Season well and bring to a boil. Cover and simmer for about 20 minutes until all the vegetables are tender. Adjust the seasoning before serving, sprinkled with the chopped peanuts.

Corn and Crabmeat Soup

It's very easy to prepare this popular first course from Chinese restaurants at home. Just be sure to use canned creamed corn to achieve the correct consistency.

INGREDIENTS

Serves 4

4 ounces crabmeat

¹/₂ teaspoon minced fresh ginger root

2 tablespoons milk

1 tablespoon cornstarch

2 egg whites

2¹/₂ cups vegetable stock

8-ounce can creamed corn

salt and freshly ground black pepper

chopped scallions, to garnish

3 In a wok or saucepan, bring the vegetable stock to a boil. Add the creamed corn and return to a boil.

4 Stir in the crabmeat-and-egg-white mixture, adjust the seasoning, and stir slowly until well blended. Serve garnished with chopped scallions.

1 Flake the crabmeat and mix it with the ginger in a bowl. In another bowl, stir the milk and cornstarch together until smooth.

2 Beat the egg whites until frothy, add the milk and cornstarch mixture, and beat again until smooth. Blend with the crabmeat.

VARIATION

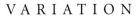

If you prefer, use coarsely chopped chicken breast instead of crabmeat.

Won-Ton Soup

In China, won-ton soup is served as a snack, or dim sum, rather than as a soup course during a large meal.

INGREDIENTS

Serves 4

generous 1 cup roughly chopped pork,
    not too lean

½ cup minced shelled shrimp

1 teaspoon light brown sugar

1 tablespoon Chinese rice wine or
    dry sherry

1 tablespoon light soy sauce

1 teaspoon minced scallions

1 teaspoon minced fresh ginger root

24 ready-made won-ton wrappers

about 3 cups stock

1 tablespoon light soy sauce

finely chopped scallions, to garnish

1 In a bowl, thoroughly mix the chopped pork and shrimp with the sugar, rice wine or sherry, soy sauce, scallions and ginger; set aside for 25 to 30 minutes for the flavors to blend.

2 Place about 1 teaspoon of the pork mixture in the center of each won-ton wrapper.

3 Wet the edges of each filled won-ton wrapper with a little water and press them together with your fingers to seal. Fold each won-ton bundle over.

4 To cook, bring the stock to a rolling boil in a wok. Add the won-tons and boil for 4 to 5 minutes. Season with the soy sauce and add the scallions.

5 Transfer to individual soup bowls and serve piping hot.

HEARTY LUNCH
& SUPPER
SOUPS

Winter Vegetable Soup

No fewer than eight varieties of vegetables are packed into this hearty and nutritious soup.

INGREDIENTS

Serves 8

1 medium Savoy cabbage, quartered
   and cored
2 tablespoons corn oil
4 carrots, finely sliced
2 celery stalks, finely sliced
2 parsnips, diced
1½ quarts chicken stock
3 potatoes, diced
2 zucchini, sliced
1 small red bell pepper, seeded and diced
2 cups cauliflower flowerets
2 tomatoes, seeded and diced
½ teaspoon fresh thyme leaves, or
   ¼ teaspoon dried thyme
2 tablespoons chopped fresh parsley
salt and freshly ground black pepper

1 Using a sharp knife, slice the cabbage quarters into thin strips across the leaves.

2 Heat the oil in a large saucepan. Add the cabbage, carrots, celery, and parsnips and cook over medium heat for 10 to 15 minutes, stirring frequently.

3 Stir the stock into the vegetables and bring to a boil, skimming off any foam from the surface.

4 Add the potatoes, zucchini, pepper, cauliflower, and tomatoes with the herbs and salt and pepper to taste. Return to a boil. Lower the heat to low, cover the pan, and simmer for 15 to 20 minutes until the vegetables are tender. Serve hot.

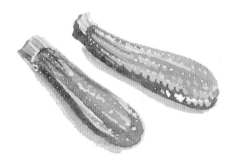

Vegetable and Herb Chowder

V

A medley of fresh vegetables and herbs combines to make a delicious lunchtime soup.

INGREDIENTS

Serves 4

2 tablespoons butter

1 onion, minced

1 leek, finely sliced

1 celery stalk, diced

1 yellow or green bell pepper, seeded and diced

2 tablespoons chopped fresh parsley

1 tablespoon all-purpose flour

1¼ quarts vegetable stock

2½ cups diced potatoes

a few sprigs of fresh thyme, or ½ teaspoon dried thyme

1 bay leaf

1 cup young green beans, thinly sliced

½ cup milk

salt and freshly ground black pepper

1 Melt the butter in a heavy-bottomed saucepan or flameproof casserole. Add the onion, leek, celery, yellow or green pepper, and parsley. Cover and cook slowly over low heat until the vegetables are soft.

2 Add the flour and stir until well blended. Slowly add the stock, stirring to combine. Bring to a boil, stirring frequently.

3 Add the potatoes, thyme, and bay leaf. Lower the heat and simmer, uncovered, for about 10 minutes.

4 Add the beans and simmer for 10 to 15 minutes longer until all the vegetables are tender.

5 Stir in the milk. Season with salt and pepper and heat through. Before serving, discard the thyme stalks and bay leaf. Serve hot.

Vegetable Soup with Coconut

V

The coconut gives a delicious flavor to this fine vegetable soup.

INGREDIENTS

Serves 4

2 tablespoons butter or margarine

½ red onion, minced

generous 1 cup each diced turnip, sweet
    potato, and pumpkin

1 teaspoon dried marjoram

½ teaspoon ground ginger

¼ teaspoon ground cinnamon

1 tablespoon chopped scallion

1 quart well-flavored vegetable stock

2 tablespoons slivered almonds

1 fresh chili, seeded and chopped

1 teaspoon sugar

1 ounce creamed coconut

salt and freshly ground black pepper

chopped fresh cilantro, to garnish
    (optional)

1 Melt the butter or margarine in a large, nonstick saucepan. Add the onion and fry for 4 to 5 minutes. Add the diced vegetables and fry for 3 to 4 minutes longer.

2 Add the marjoram, ginger, cinnamon, scallion, and salt and pepper to taste. Fry over low heat for about 10 minutes, stirring frequently.

3 Add the vegetable stock, slivered almonds, chili and sugar and stir well to mix. Cover and simmer for 10 to 15 minutes until the vegetables are just tender.

4 Grate the creamed coconut into the soup and stir well. Spoon into warm bowls and sprinkle with chopped cilantro, if liked. Serve at once.

Fava Bean and Rice Soup

This thick soup makes the most of fresh fava beans while they are in season, but it also works well with frozen beans for the rest of the year.

INGREDIENTS

Serves 4

2¼ pounds fava beans in their pods, or
    scant 3 cups shelled frozen fava
    beans, thawed

6 tablespoons olive oil

1 onion, minced

2 tomatoes, peeled and finely chopped

1 cup arborio or other
    nonparboiled rice

2 tablespoons butter

1 quart boiling water

salt and freshly ground black pepper

grated Parmesan cheese, to serve
    (optional)

1 Bring a large pan of water to the boil and blanch the beans, fresh or frozen, for 3 to 4 minutes. Rinse under cold water. If using fresh beans, peel off the skins.

2 Heat the oil in a large saucepan. Add the onion and cook over low to medium heat until it is soft. Stir in the beans and cook for about 5 minutes, stirring to coat them with the oil.

3 Season with salt and pepper. Add the tomatoes and cook for 5 minutes longer, stirring often. Add the rice and cook for 1 to 2 minutes longer, stirring constantly.

4 Add the butter and stir until it melts. Pour in the water, a little at a time. Adjust the seasoning to taste. Continue cooking until the rice is tender. Serve with grated Parmesan, if liked.

Fresh Tomato and Bean Soup

V

This is a rich, chunky tomato soup, with beans and cilantro. Serve with olive ciabatta bread.

Serves 4

2 pounds ripe plum tomatoes

2 tablespoons olive oil

2 cups roughly chopped onions

2 garlic cloves, crushed

3¾ cups vegetable stock

2 tablespoons sun-dried tomato paste

2 teaspoons paprika

1 tablespoon cornstarch

15-ounce can cannellini beans, rinsed
    and drained

2 tablespoons chopped fresh cilantro

salt and freshly ground black pepper

olive ciabatta bread, to serve

1 First, peel the tomatoes. Using a sharp knife, make a small cross in each one and place in a bowl. Pour enough boiling water over to cover and leave to stand for 30 to 60 seconds.

2 Drain the tomatoes and, when they are cool enough to handle, peel off the skins. Quarter them and then cut each piece in half again.

3 Heat the oil in a large saucepan. Add the onions and garlic and cook for 3 minutes, or until just beginning to become soft.

4 Add the tomatoes to the onions and stir in the stock, sun-dried tomato paste and paprika. Season with a little salt and pepper. Bring to a boil and simmer for 10 minutes.

5 Mix the cornstarch to a paste with 2 tablespoons water. Stir the beans into the soup with the cornstarch paste. Cook for 5 minutes longer.

6 Adjust the seasoning and stir in the chopped cilantro just before serving with olive ciabatta bread.

Cauliflower, Flageolet, and Fennel Seed Soup

The sweet, anise-licorice flavor of the fennel seeds gives a delicious edge to this hearty soup.

INGREDIENTS

Serves 4 to 6

1 tablespoon olive oil

1 garlic clove, crushed

1 onion, chopped

2 teaspoons fennel seeds

1 cauliflower, cut into small flowerets

2 x 14-ounce cans flageolet beans, drained and rinsed

1¼ quarts vegetable stock or water

salt and freshly ground black pepper

chopped fresh parsley, to garnish

toasted slices of French bread, to serve

3 Bring the soup to a boil. Lower the heat and simmer for about 10 minutes, or until the cauliflower is tender. Pour the soup into a blender or food processor and blend until smooth.

4 Stir in the remaining beans and season to taste. Reheat and pour into bowls. Sprinkle with chopped parsley and serve with toasted slices of French bread.

1 Heat the olive oil. Add the garlic, onion, and fennel seeds and cook slowly for 5 minutes, or until soft.

2 Add the cauliflower flowerets, half the beans, and all the vegetable stock or water.

Beet and Lima Bean Soup

This soup is a simplified version of borscht and is prepared in a fraction of the time. Serve with a spoonful of sour cream and a scattering of chopped fresh parsley.

INGREDIENTS

Serves 4

2 tablespoons vegetable oil

1 onion, sliced

1 teaspoon caraway seeds

finely grated rind of ½ orange

generous 2 cups grated cooked beets

1¼ cups beef stock or rassol
   (see Cook's Tip)

14-ounce can lima beans, drained
   and rinsed

1 tablespoon wine vinegar

4 tablespoons sour cream

4 tablespoons chopped fresh parsley,
   to garnish

1 Heat the oil in a large saucepan. Add the onion, caraway seeds, and orange peel and cook until soft but not colored.

2 Add the beets, stock or rassol, lima beans, and vinegar and simmer over low heat for 10 minutes longer.

3 Divide the soup between 4 bowls, add a spoonful of sour cream to each, and scatter with chopped parsley. Serve at once.

COOK'S TIP

Rassol is a beet broth, which is used to impart a strong beet color and flavor to dishes. You are most likely to find it in kosher food stores.

Spicy Bean Soup

A filling soup made with two kinds of beans flavored with cumin.

Serves 6 to 8

1 cup dried black beans, soaked overnight
    and drained
1 cup dried kidney beans, soaked
    overnight and drained
2 bay leaves
2 tablespoons olive or vegetable oil
3 carrots, chopped
1 onion, chopped
1 celery stalk, chopped
1 garlic clove, crushed
1 teaspoon ground cumin
$1/4$ to $1/2$ teaspoon cayenne pepper
$1/2$ teaspoon dried oregano
$1/4$ cup red wine
5 cups beef stock
1 cup water
salt and freshly ground black pepper

For the garnish
sour cream
chopped fresh cilantro

1 Put the black beans and kidney beans in two separate pans with enough cold water to cover and a bay leaf in each. Boil rapidly for 10–15 minutes.

2 Reduce the heat and cover the pans. Simmer for 1 hour until the beans are tender, then drain.

3 Heat the oil in a large flameproof casserole. Add the carrots, onion, celery, and garlic and cook over low heat for 8 to 10 minutes, stirring, until soft. Stir in the cumin, cayenne, oregano, and salt to taste.

4 Add the wine, stock, and water and stir to mix all the ingredients together. Remove the bay leaves from the cooked beans and add the beans to the casserole.

5 Bring to a boil. Lower the heat, cover the pan, and simmer for about 20 minutes, stirring occasionally.

6 Transfer half the soup, including most of the solids, to a food processor or blender. Process until smooth. Return to the pan and stir well.

7 Reheat the soup and adjust the seasoning to taste. Serve hot, garnished with sour cream and chopped cilantro.

Black and White Bean Soup

Although this soup takes a while to prepare, the results are so stunning that it is well worth the effort.

INGREDIENTS

Serves 8

2 cups dried black beans, soaked overnight and drained

2½ quarts water

6 garlic cloves, crushed

2 cups dried white beans, soaked overnight and drained

6 tablespoons balsamic vinegar

4 jalapeño peppers, seeded and chopped

6 scallions, minced

juice of 1 lime

¼ cup olive oil

¼ cup chopped fresh cilantro, plus extra to garnish

salt and freshly ground black pepper

1 Place the black beans in a large saucepan with half the water and garlic and bring to a boil. Lower the heat to low, cover the pan, and simmer for about 1½ hours until the beans are soft.

2 Meanwhile, put the white beans in another saucepan with the remaining water and garlic and bring to a boil. Lower the heat, cover the pan, and simmer for about 1 hour until soft.

3 Purée the cooked white beans in a food processor or blender. Stir in the vinegar, jalapeños, and half the scallions. Return to the saucepan and reheat slowly.

4 Purée the cooked black beans in the food processor or blender. Return to the saucepan and stir in the lime juice, olive oil, cilantro, and remaining scallions. Reheat slowly.

5 Season both soups with salt and black pepper. To serve, place a ladleful of both puréed soups in each bowl, side by side. Swirl the 2 soups together with a toothpick or skewer. Garnish with fresh cilantro.

V

Pistou

Serve this delicious vegetable soup from Nice, in the south of France, with a sun-dried tomato pesto and fresh Parmesan cheese.

INGREDIENTS

Serves 4

1 zucchini, diced

1 small potato, diced

1 shallot, chopped

1 carrot, diced

8-ounce can chopped tomatoes

1¼ quarts vegetable stock

½ cup thin green beans cut into
    ½-inch pieces

½ cup frozen small peas

½ cup small pasta shapes

4–6 tablespoons pesto, either homemade
    or store bought

1 tablespoon sun-dried tomato paste

salt and freshly ground black pepper

grated Parmesan cheese, to serve

1 Place the zucchini, potato, shallot, carrot, and tomatoes in a large pan. Add the vegetable stock and season with salt and pepper. Bring to a boil. Cover and simmer for 20 minutes.

2 Add the green beans, peas and pasta shapes. Cook for 10 minutes longer, until the pasta is tender.

3 Taste the soup and adjust the seasoning as necessary. Ladle the soup into individual bowls. Mix together the pesto and sun-dried tomato paste, and stir a spoonful into each serving.

4 Hand around a bowl of grated Parmesan cheese for sprinkling into each bowl.

Ribollita

Ribollita is like minestrone, but includes beans instead of pasta. In Italy, this is traditionally served ladled over bread and a rich green vegetable, although you can omit this for a lighter version.

INGREDIENTS

Serves 6 to 8

3 tablespoons olive oil

2 onions, chopped

2 carrots, sliced

4 garlic cloves, crushed

2 celery stalks, finely sliced

1 fennel bulb, trimmed and chopped

2 large zucchini, finely sliced

14-ounce can crushed tomatoes

2 tablespoons pesto, either homemade
  or store bought

3¾ cups vegetable stock

14-ounce can haricot or borlotti beans,
  drained

salt and freshly ground black pepper

To serve

1 pound young spinach

1 tablespoon extra-virgin olive oil, plus
  extra for drizzling

6 to 8 slices white bread

Parmesan cheese shavings (optional)

1 Heat the oil in a large saucepan. Add the onions, carrots, garlic, celery, and fennel and fry slowly for 10 minutes. Add the zucchini slices and fry for 2 minutes longer.

2 Add the crushed tomatoes, pesto, stock, and beans and bring to a boil. Lower the heat, cover, and simmer for 25 to 30 minutes until all the vegetables are tender. Season with salt and freshly ground black pepper to taste.

3 To serve, fry the spinach in the oil for 2 minutes, or until it wilts. Spoon over the bread in soup bowls and ladle the soup over the spinach. Serve with extra olive oil for drizzling onto the soup and Parmesan cheese to sprinkle on top, if liked.

Plantain and Corn Soup

Here the sweetness of the corn kernels and plantains is offset by a little chili to create an unusual soup.

INGREDIENTS

Serves 4

2 tablespoons butter or margarine

1 onion, minced

1 garlic clove, crushed

2 cups peeled and sliced yellow plantains

1 large tomato, peeled and chopped

1 cup whole corn kernels

1 teaspoon dried tarragon, crushed

3¾ cups vegetable or chicken stock

1 fresh green chili, seeded and chopped

a pinch of freshly grated nutmeg

salt and freshly ground black pepper

1 Melt the butter or margarine in a saucepan over medium heat. Add the onion and garlic and fry for a few minutes until the onion is soft.

2 Add the plantains, tomato, and corn kernels and cook for 5 minutes longer.

3 Add the tarragon, stock, green chili and salt and freshly ground black pepper. Simmer for 10 minutes, or until the plantain is tender. Stir in the grated nutmeg and serve at once.

Groundnut Soup

Groundnuts, the African name for peanuts, are widely used in sauces in African cooking. You'll find groundnut paste in health food stores—it makes a wonderfully rich soup. Look for white yams in Latin American food stores.

INGREDIENTS

Serves 4

3 tablespoons groundnut paste or peanut butter

1½ quarts stock or water

2 tablespoons tomato paste

1 onion, chopped

2 slices fresh ginger root

¼ teaspoon dried thyme

1 bay leaf

cayenne pepper

1½ cups diced white yam

10 small okras, trimmed (optional)

salt

1 Place the groundnut paste or peanut butter in a bowl. Add 1¼ cups of the stock or water and the tomato paste and blend together to make a smooth paste.

2 Spoon the nut mixture into a saucepan. Add the onion, ginger, thyme, bay leaf, cayenne pepper, salt to taste, and the remaining stock.

3 Heat slowly until simmering, then cook for 1 hour, whisking from time to time to prevent the nut mixture from sticking.

4 Add the white yam and cook for 10 minutes longer. Add the okra, if using, and simmer until both vegetables are tender. Serve at once.

V

Italian Arugula and Potato Soup

This filling and hearty soup is based on a traditional Italian peasant recipe. If arugula is unavailable, watercress or baby spinach leaves make equally delicious alternatives.

INGREDIENTS

Serves 4

2 pounds new potatoes

3¾ cups well-flavored vegetable stock

1 medium carrot

4 ounces arugula

½ teaspoon cayenne pepper

½ loaf stale ciabatta bread, torn into chunks

4 garlic cloves, thinly sliced

4 tablespoons olive oil

salt and freshly ground black pepper

3 Add the cayenne pepper, salt and black pepper to taste, and the chunks of bread. Remove the pan from the heat, cover, and leave to stand for about 10 minutes.

4 Meanwhile, sauté the garlic in the olive oil until golden brown. Pour the soup into bowls and add a little of the sautéed garlic to each bowl. Serve at once.

1 Dice the potatoes. Place them in a saucepan with the stock and a little salt and bring to a boil. Simmer for 10 minutes.

2 Finely dice the carrot and add to the potatoes and stock. Tear the arugula leaves and drop into the pan. Simmer for 15 minutes longer until the vegetables are tender.

Czech Fish Soup with Dumplings

Use a variety of whatever fish is available in this soup, such as perch, catfish, cod, or snapper. The basis of the dumplings is the same whether you use semolina or flour.

INGREDIENTS

Serves 4 to 8

3 rindless bacon slices, diced

1½ pounds assorted fresh fish, skinned, boned and diced

1 tablespoon paprika, plus extra to garnish

1½ quarts fish stock or water

3 firm tomatoes, peeled and chopped

4 waxy potatoes, peeled and grated

1–2 teaspoons chopped fresh marjoram, plus extra to garnish

For the dumplings

½ cup semolina or all-purpose flour

1 egg, beaten

3 tablespoons milk or water

generous pinch of salt

1 tablespoon chopped fresh parsley

1 Dry-fry the diced bacon in a large pan until pale golden brown. Add the pieces of assorted fish and fry for 1 to 2 minutes, taking care not to break up the pieces of fish.

2 Sprinkle in the paprika, pour in the fish stock or water, and bring to a boil. Lower the heat and simmer for 10 minutes.

3 Stir the tomatoes, grated potato, and marjoram into the pan. Cook for 10 minutes, stirring occasionally.

4 Meanwhile, make the dumplings by mixing all the ingredients together. Leave to stand, covered with plastic wrap for 5 to 10 minutes.

5 Drop spoonfuls of the dumpling mixture into the soup and cook for 10 minutes. Serve hot with a little marjoram and paprika.

Yellow Broth

This is one of many versions of this famous Irish soup, which is both thickened with, and given its flavor by, steel-cut oats.

INGREDIENTS

Serves 4

2 tablespoons butter
1 onion, minced
1 celery stalk, minced
1 carrot, finely chopped
2 tablespoons all-purpose flour
3¾ cups chicken stock
¼ cup medium steel-cut oats
1½ cups chopped spinach
2 tablespoons cream
salt and freshly ground black pepper
chopped fresh parsley, to garnish
(optional)

1 Melt the butter in a large saucepan. Add the onion, celery, and carrot and cook for about 2 minutes until the onion begins to become soft.

2 Stir in the flour and cook slowly for 1 minute longer, stirring constantly. Pour in the chicken stock and bring to a boil. Lower the heat, cover, and simmer for 30 minutes until the vegetables are tender.

3 Stir in the oats and chopped spinach and cook for 15 minutes longer, stirring from time to time.

4 Stir in the cream and season well. Serve garnished with chopped fresh parsley, if using.

Split Pea and Pumpkin Soup

V

Corned beef is often used in this creamy pea soup. This is the vegetarian version, however.

INGREDIENTS

Serves 4

1 cup split peas

1¼ quarts water

2 tablespoons butter

1 onion, minced

1½ cups chopped pumpkin

3 tomatoes, peeled and chopped

1 teaspoon dried tarragon, crushed

1 tablespoon chopped fresh cilantro

½ teaspoon ground cumin

1 vegetable bouillon cube, crumbled

cayenne pepper, to taste

sprigs of fresh cilantro, to garnish

1 Soak the split peas overnight in enough water to cover them completely; drain. Place the split peas in a large saucepan, add the water, and boil for about 30 minutes until tender.

2 In a separate pan, melt the butter and sauté the onion until soft but not brown.

3 Add the pumpkin, tomatoes, tarragon, cilantro, cumin, vegetable bouillon cube, and cayenne pepper. Bring to a boil over high heat.

4 Stir the vegetable mixture into the cooked split peas and their liquid. Simmer for about 20 minutes, or until the vegetables are tender. If the soup is too thick, add another ⅔ cup water. Serve hot, garnished with sprigs of cilantro.

V

Green Lentil Soup

Lentil soup is an eastern Mediterranean classic, varying in its spiciness according to region. Red or Puy lentils make an equally good substitute for the green lentils used in this version.

INGREDIENTS

Serves 4 to 6

1⅓ cups green lentils

5 tablespoons olive oil

3 onions, minced

2 garlic cloves, finely sliced

2 teaspoons cumin seeds, crushed

¼ teaspoon ground turmeric

2½ cups vegetable stock

2½ cups water

salt and freshly ground black pepper

2 tablespoons roughly chopped fresh cilantro, to garnish

warm crusty bread, to serve

1 Put the lentils in a saucepan and cover with cold water. Bring to a boil and boil rapidly for 10 minutes; drain.

2 Heat 2 tablespoons of the oil in a pan. Add 2 of the onions, the garlic, cumin, and turmeric and fry for 3 minutes, stirring. Add the lentils, stock, and water and bring to a boil. Lower the heat, cover, and simmer for 30 minutes until the lentils are soft.

3 Heat the remaining oil. Add the third onion and fry until golden brown, stirring frequently.

4 Use a potato masher to lightly mash the lentils and make the soup pulpy in texture. Reheat slowly and season with salt and freshly ground pepper to taste.

5 Pour the soup into bowls. Stir some fresh cilantro in with the fried onion and scatter the rest over the soup as a garnish. Serve with warm crusty bread.

> ### COOK'S TIP
> ❧
>
> Lentils do not need to be soaked before cooking.

Lentil Soup with Rosemary

A classic rustic Italian soup flavored with rosemary, this is delicious served with garlic bread.

INGREDIENTS

Serves 4

1 cup dried green or brown lentils

3 tablespoons extra-virgin olive oil

3 bacon slices, cut into small dice

1 onion, minced

2 celery stalks, minced

2 carrots, minced

2 sprigs of fresh rosemary, minced

2 bay leaves

14-ounce can plum tomatoes

1¾ quarts vegetable stock

salt and freshly ground black pepper

fresh bay leaves and sprigs of fresh
    rosemary, to garnish

1 Place the lentils in a bowl and cover with cold water. Leave to soak for at least 2 hours; rinse and drain well.

2 Heat the oil in a large saucepan. Add the bacon and cook for about 3 minutes. Stir in the onion and cook for 5 minutes until soft. Stir in the celery, carrots, rosemary, bay leaves, and lentils. Toss over the heat for 1 minute until thoroughly coated in the oil.

3 Tip in the tomatoes and stock, and bring to a boil. Lower the heat, half-cover the pan, and simmer for about 1 hour until the lentils are tender.

4 Remove the bay leaves and add salt and freshly ground black pepper to taste. Serve with a garnish of fresh bay leaves and sprigs of rosemary.

COOK'S TIP

Look for the small green lentils in Italian groceries or delicatessens.

V

Lentil and Pasta Soup

This rustic vegetarian soup makes a filling lunch or supper and goes well with granary or crusty Italian bread.

INGREDIENTS

Serves 4 to 6

¾ cup brown lentils

3 garlic cloves

1 quart water

3 tablespoons olive oil

2 tablespoons butter

1 onion, minced

2 celery stalks, minced

2 tablespoons sun-dried tomato paste

1¾ quarts vegetable stock

a few fresh marjoram leaves, plus extra
     to garnish

a few fresh basil leaves

leaves from 1 sprig of fresh thyme

½ cup small pasta shapes,
     such as *tubetti*

salt and freshly ground black pepper

1 Put the lentils in a large saucepan. Smash one of the garlic cloves (there's no need to peel it first) and add it to the lentils. Pour in the water and bring to a boil. Lower the heat to a slow simmer and simmer for about 20 minutes, stirring occasionally, until the lentils are just tender.

2 Tip the lentils into a strainer and remove the cooked garlic clove; set it aside.

3 Rinse the lentils in cold water; leave them to drain. Heat 2 tablespoons of the oil with half of the butter in a large saucepan. Add the onion and celery and cook over low heat, for 5–7 minutes, stirring frequently, until soft.

COOK'S TIP

Use green lentils instead of brown, if you like, but the orange or red ones are not good for this soup because they become too mushy.

4 Crush the remaining garlic and peel and mash the reserved cooked garlic clove. Stir into the vegetables with the remaining oil, the tomato paste and lentils. Add the stock, herbs, and salt and pepper to taste, and bring to a boil, stirring. Lower the heat and simmer for 30 minutes, stirring occasionally.

5 Add the pasta and bring to a boil, stirring. Simmer, stirring frequently, for 7 to 8 minutes, or according to the directions on the package, until the pasta is *al dente*. Add the remaining butter and adjust the seasoning. Serve hot in warm bowls, garnished with marjoram leaves.

Roasted Tomato and Pasta Soup

When the only tomatoes you can buy are not particularly flavorsome, make this soup. The roasting compensates for any lack of flavor in the tomatoes, and the soup has a wonderful, smoky taste.

INGREDIENTS

Serves 4

1 pound ripe Italian plum tomatoes, halved lengthwise

1 large red bell pepper, quartered lengthwise and seeded

1 large red onion, quartered lengthwise

2 garlic cloves, unpeeled

1 tablespoon olive oil

1¼ quarts vegetable stock or water

a good pinch of sugar

scant 1 cup small pasta shapes, such as *tubetti* or small macaroni

salt and freshly ground black pepper

fresh basil leaves, to garnish

1 Heat the oven to 375°F. Spread out the tomatoes, red pepper, onion, and garlic in a roasting pan and drizzle with the olive oil. Roast for 30 to 40 minutes until the vegetables are soft and charred, stirring and turning them halfway through cooking.

2 Tip the vegetables into a food processor, add about 1 cup of the stock or water, and process until puréed. Scrape into a strainer placed over a large saucepan and press the purée through into the pan.

3 Add the remaining stock or water, the sugar and salt and pepper to taste. Bring to a boil.

4 Add the pasta and simmer for 7 to 8 minutes, or according to the directions on the package, stirring frequently, until *al dente*. Taste and adjust the seasoning with salt and freshly ground black pepper. Serve hot in warm bowls, garnished with the fresh basil leaves.

COOK'S TIP

You can roast the vegetables in advance and let them cool, then leave them in a covered bowl in the refrigerator overnight before puréeing.

Tiny Pasta in Broth

In Italy, this soup is often served with bread for a light supper.

Serves 4

1¼ quarts beef stock

¾ cup small soup pasta, such as *stellette*

2 pieces bottled roasted red bell pepper, about 2 ounces

salt and freshly ground black pepper

grated Parmesan cheese, to serve

1 Bring the beef stock to a boil in a large saucepan. Add salt and pepper to taste and drop in the soup pasta. Stir well and bring the stock back to a boil.

2 Lower the heat and simmer for 7 to 8 minutes, or according to the package directions, until the pasta is *al dente*. Stir often during cooking to prevent the pasta shapes from sticking together.

3 Drain the pieces of bottled roasted pepper and dice them finely. Place them in the bottom of 4 warm soup bowls; set aside.

4 Taste the soup and adjust the seasoning. Ladle into the soup plates and serve immediately, with grated Parmesan handed round separately.

Little Stuffed Hats in Broth

This soup is served in northern Italy on Santo Stefano (St. Stephen's Day, the day after Christmas) and on New Year's Day. It makes a welcome change from all the celebration food, the day before. It is traditionally made with the Christmas capon carcass, but chicken stock works equally well.

Serves 4

1¼ quarts chicken stock

1 cup fresh or dried *cappelletti*

2 tablespoons dry white wine (optional)

about 1 tablespoon finely chopped fresh flat-leaf parsley (optional)

salt and freshly ground black pepper

about 2 tablespoons grated Parmesan cheese, to serve

1 Pour the chicken stock into a large saucepan and bring to a boil. Add a little salt and pepper to taste and drop in the pasta.

2 Stir well and return to a boil. Lower the heat to a simmer and cook according to the directions on the package, until the pasta is *al dente*. Stir frequently during cooking to make sure the pasta cooks evenly.

3 Swirl in the wine and parsley, if using, then taste and adjust the seasoning. Ladle into 4 warm soup bowls. Sprinkle with grated Parmesan. Serve immediately.

COOK'S TIP

Cappelletti is just another name for tortellini, which come from Romagna. You can either buy them or make your own.

Pasta and Chick-Pea Soup

This is a simple, country-style, filling soup. The different shapes of the pasta and the beans complement each other beautifully.

INGREDIENTS

Serves 4 to 6

4 tablespoons olive oil

1 onion, minced

2 carrots, minced

2 celery stalks, finely chopped

14-ounce can chick-peas, rinsed and drained

7-ounce can cannellini beans, rinsed and drained

2/3 cup passata (puréed tomatoes)

1/2 cup water

1 1/2 quarts vegetable or chicken stock

1 sprig of fresh rosemary, plus a few leaves to garnish

scant 2 cups dried *conchiglie*

salt and freshly ground black pepper

shavings of Parmesan cheese, to serve

1 Heat the oil in a large saucepan. Add the chopped vegetables and cook over low heat, stirring frequently, for 5 to 7 minutes.

2 Add the chick-peas and cannellini beans, stir well to mix, and cook for 5 minutes. Stir in the passata and water. Cook, stirring, for 2 to 3 minutes.

3 Add 2 cups of the stock, the rosemary sprig, and salt and freshly ground black pepper to taste and bring to a boil. Lower the heat, cover, and simmer, stirring occasionally, for 1 hour.

VARIATIONS
~

You can use other pasta shapes, but *conchiglie* are ideal because they scoop up the chick-peas and beans. Crush 1 or 2 garlic cloves and fry them with the vegetables, if you like.

4 Pour in the remaining stock, add the pasta, and bring to a boil. Lower the heat and simmer for 7 to 8 minutes, or according to the directions on the package, until the pasta is *al dente*. Remove the rosemary sprig. Serve the soup sprinkled with rosemary leaves and Parmesan shavings.

Chick-Pea and Parsley Soup

Parsley and a hint of lemon bring freshness to chick-peas.

INGREDIENTS

Serves 6

1⅓ cups dried chick-peas, soaked
    overnight

1 small onion

1 bunch of fresh parsley, about 1½ ounces

2 tablespoons olive and sunflower oils,
    mixed

1¼ quarts chicken stock

juice of ½ lemon

salt and freshly ground black pepper

lemon wedges and finely pared strips of
    peel, to garnish

1 Drain the chick-peas and rinse under cold water. Cook them in boiling water for 1 to 1½ hours until tender; drain and peel.

2 Place the onion and parsley in a food processor or blender and process until finely chopped.

3 Heat the olive and sunflower oils in a saucepan or flame-proof casserole. Add the onion mixture and fry for about 4 minutes over low heat until the onion is slightly soft.

4 Add the chick-peas and cook slowly for 1 to 2 minutes. Pour in the stock and season well. Bring the soup to a boil. Cover and simmer for 20 minutes.

5 Leave the soup to cool a little and then mash the chick-peas with a fork until the soup is thick, but still quite chunky.

6 Reheat the soup and add the lemon juice. Serve garnished with lemon wedges and peel.

Chick-Pea and Spinach Soup with Garlic

This delicious, thick, and creamy soup is richly flavored and perfect for vegetarians.

INGREDIENTS

Serves 4

2 tablespoons olive oil

4 garlic cloves, crushed

1 onion, roughly chopped

2 teaspoons ground cumin

2 teaspoons ground coriander

1¼ quarts vegetable stock

2½ cups finely chopped potatoes

15-ounce can chick-peas, drained

1 tablespoon cornstarch

⅔ cup heavy cream

2 tablespoons light tahini

3½ cups shredded spinach

cayenne pepper

salt and freshly ground black pepper

2 Stir in the ground cumin and coriander and cook for 1 minute. Add the stock and potatoes and bring to a boil. Simmer for 10 minutes.

3 Add the chick-peas and simmer for 5 minutes longer or until the potatoes are just tender.

4 Blend together the cornstarch, cream, tahini, and plenty of seasoning. Stir into the soup with the spinach and bring to a boil, stirring. Lower the heat and simmer for 2 minutes. Adjust the seasoning with salt, pepper and cayenne pepper to taste. Serve sprinkled with a little extra cayenne pepper.

1 Heat the oil in a large saucepan. Add the garlic and onion and fry for about 5 minutes, or until the onion is soft and golden brown.

COOK'S TIP
∼

Tahini is sesame seed paste and is available from health-food stores and supermarkets.

Eastern European Chick-Pea Soup

Chick-peas form part of the staple diet in the Balkans, where this soup originates. It is economical to make, and is a hearty and satisfying dish.

INGREDIENTS

Serves 4 to 6

5 cups chick-peas, soaked overnight

2¼ quarts vegetable stock

3 large waxy potatoes, cut into bite-size chunks

¼ cup olive oil

8 ounces spinach leaves

salt and freshly ground black pepper

spicy sausage, cooked (optional)

1 Drain the chick-peas and rinse under cold water. Place in a large pan with the vegetable stock and bring to a boil. Lower the heat and cook slowly for about 1 hour.

2 Add the potatoes, olive oil, and salt and pepper to taste and cook for 20 minutes until the potatoes are tender.

3 Add the spinach and sliced, cooked sausages (if using) 5 minutes before the end of cooking. Serve the soup in warm soup bowls.

Corn and Scallop Chowder

Fresh corn is ideal for this chowder, although canned or frozen corn kernels also work well. This soup is almost a meal in itself and makes a perfect lunch dish.

INGREDIENTS

Serves 4 to 6

2 corn cobs or generous 1 cup frozen or
   canned corn kernels

2½ cups milk

1 tablespoon butter or margarine

1 small leek or onion, chopped

¼ cup finely chopped smoked bacon

1 small garlic clove, crushed

1 small green bell pepper, seeded
   and diced

1 celery stalk, chopped

1 medium potato, diced

1 tablespoon all-purpose flour

1¼ cups chicken or vegetable stock

4 scallops

4 ounces cooked fresh mussels

a pinch of paprika

⅔ cup light cream (optional)

salt and freshly ground black pepper

1 Using a sharp knife, slice down the corn cobs to remove the kernels. Place half the kernels in a food processor or blender and process with a little of the milk; set the other half aside.

2 Melt the butter or margarine in a large saucepan. Add the leek or onion, bacon, and garlic and fry for 4 to 5 minutes until the leek is soft but not brown. Add the green pepper, celery, and potato and sweat over low heat for 3 to 4 minutes longer, stirring frequently.

3 Stir in the flour and cook for 1 to 2 minutes until the mixture turns golden and frothy. Stir in the milk and corn mixture, stock, the remaining milk and corn kernels and seasoning.

4 Bring to a boil. Lower the heat and simmer, partially covered, for 15 to 20 minutes until the vegetables are tender.

5 Pull the corals away from the scallops and slice the white flesh into ¼-inch slices. Stir the scallops into the soup and cook for 4 minutes. Stir in the corals, mussels, and paprika and heat through for a few minutes. Stir in the cream, if using. Check the seasoning and serve.

Clam Chowder

A traditional chowder from New England. The mixture of clams and pork, with potatoes and cream, is rich and utterly delicious.

INGREDIENTS

Serves 8

48 clams, scrubbed

1½ quarts water

¼ cup finely diced salt pork
   or bacon

3 onions, minced

1 bay leaf

3 potatoes, diced

2 cups milk, warmed

1 cup light cream

salt and freshly ground black pepper

chopped fresh parsley, to garnish

1 Rinse the clams well in cold water; drain. Place them in a deep pan with the water and bring to a boil. Cover and steam for about 10 minutes until the shells open. Remove from the heat.

2 When the clams have cooled slightly, remove them from their shells. Discard any clams that have not opened. Chop the clams coarsely. Strain the cooking liquid through a strainer lined with cheesecloth and reserve.

3 In a large, heavy saucepan, fry the salt pork or bacon until it renders its fat and begins to brown. Add the onions and cook over low heat for 8 to 10 minutes until softened.

4 Stir in the bay leaf, potatoes, and clam cooking liquid. Bring to a boil and boil for 5 to 10 minutes.

5 Stir in the chopped clams. Continue to cook until the potatoes are tender, stirring from time to time. Season to taste.

6 Stir in the warm milk and cream and heat very slowly for 5 minutes longer. Discard the bay leaf; adjust the seasoning. Serve sprinkled with chopped fresh parsley.

Spiced Mussel Soup

Chunky and colorful, this Turkish fish soup is like a chowder in its consistency. It is flavored with harissa sauce, which is more familiar in north African cookery.

Serves 6

3 to 3½ pounds fresh mussels

⅔ cup dry white wine

2 tablespoons olive oil

1 onion, minced

2 garlic cloves, crushed

2 celery stalks, finely sliced

bunch of scallions, finely sliced

1 potato, diced

1½ teaspoons harissa sauce

3 tomatoes, peeled and diced

3 tablespoons chopped fresh parsley

freshly ground black pepper

thick plain yogurt, to serve (optional)

1 Scrub the mussels, discarding any damaged ones or open ones that do not close when tapped with a knife.

2 Bring the wine to a boil in a large saucepan. Add the mussels and cover the pan with a lid. Cook for 4 to 5 minutes until the mussels open wide: Discard any mussels that remain closed. Drain the mussels, reserving the cooking liquid. Reserve a few mussels in their shells to use as a garnish and shell the rest.

3 Heat the oil in a pan. Add the onion, garlic, celery, and scallions and fry for 5 minutes.

4 Add the shelled mussels, reserved liquid, potato, harissa sauce, and tomatoes and bring to a boil. Lower the heat, cover, simmer for 25 minutes or until the potatoes are breaking up.

5 Stir in the parsley and pepper and add the reserved mussels in their shells. Heat through for 1 minute. Serve hot with a spoonful of yogurt, if liked.

Curried Salmon Soup

Look for bars of creamed coconut in Asian grocery stores. It has a strong flavor and dissolves in liquid.

INGREDIENTS

Serves 4

4 tablespoons butter

1½ cups roughly chopped onions

2 teaspoons mild curry paste

2 cups water

⅔ cup white wine

1¼ cups heavy cream

½ cup grated creamed coconut

2½ cups finely diced potatoes

1 pound salmon fillet, skinned and cut into bite-size pieces

4 tablespoons chopped fresh flat-leaf parsley

salt and freshly ground black pepper

1 Melt the butter in a large saucepan. Add the onions and cook over low heat for 3 to 4 minutes until beginning to become soft. Add the curry paste and cook for 1 minute longer.

2 Add the water, wine, cream, creamed coconut, and a little seasoning. Bring to a boil, stirring, until the coconut dissolves smoothly.

3 Add the potatoes to the pan and simmer, covered, for about 15 minutes, or until they are almost tender: Do not let them break down into the mixture.

4 Stir the fish in gently so it does not break up. Simmer for 2 to 3 minutes until just tender. Add the parsley and adjust the seasoning. Serve at once.

Salmon Chowder

Dill is the perfect partner for salmon in this creamy soup.

Serves 4

1½ tablespoons butter or margarine

1 onion, minced

1 leek, minced

1 small fennel bulb, minced

2½ tablespoons all-purpose flour

1¾ quarts fish stock

2 potatoes, cut into ½-inch cubes

1 pound boneless, skinless salmon, cut into ¾-inch cubes

¾ cup milk

½ cup whipping cream

2 tablespoons chopped fresh dill

salt and freshly ground black pepper

1 Melt the butter or margarine in a large saucepan. Add the onion, leek, and chopped fennel and cook over medium heat for 5 to 8 minutes until soft, stirring from time to time.

2 Stir in the flour. Lower the heat to low and cook for 3 minutes, stirring occasionally.

3 Add the fish stock and potatoes. Season with salt and ground black pepper and bring to a boil. Lower the heat, cover, and simmer for about 20 minutes, or until the potatoes are tender.

4 Add the salmon and simmer for 3 to 5 minutes until it is just cooked through and flakes.

5 Stir in the milk, cream, and dill. Cook until just warmed through. Do not boil. Adjust the seasoning and serve.

Smoked Haddock and Potato Soup

The proper name for this traditional Scottish soup is cullen skink. *A* cullen *is a seatown or the port district of a town, while* skink *means stock or broth.*

INGREDIENTS

Serves 6

1 smoked haddock, about 12 ounces

1 onion, chopped

1 bouquet garni

3¾ cups water

1¼ pounds potatoes, quartered

2½ cups milk

3 tablespoons butter

salt and freshly ground black pepper

snipped fresh chives, to garnish

crusty bread, to serve

1 Put the haddock, onion, bouquet garni, and water into a large saucepan and bring to a boil. Skim the foam from the surface and cover the pan. Lower the heat and poach for 10 to 15 minutes until the haddock flakes easily.

2 Lift the haddock from the pan, using a pancake turner, and remove the skin and bones. Flake the flesh and reserve. Return the skin and bones to the pan and simmer, uncovered, for 30 minutes. Strain the stock through a strainer.

3 Return the stock to the pan, add the potatoes, and simmer for about 25 minutes, or until tender. Remove the potatoes from the pan using a slotted spoon. Add the milk to the pan and bring to a boil.

4 Meanwhile, mash the potatoes with the butter. Beat them into the liquid in the pan until thick and creamy. Add the flaked fish to the pan and adjust the seasoning. Sprinkle with chives and serve at once with crusty bread.

Smoked Cod and Okra Soup

The inspiration for this soup came from a Ghanaian recipe for okra soup. Here it is enhanced by the addition of smoked fish.

INGREDIENTS

Serves 4

2 green bananas

4 tablespoons butter or margarine

1 onion, minced

2 tomatoes, peeled and minced

4 ounces okra, trimmed

8 ounces smoked cod fillet, skinned and cut into bite-size pieces

3¾ cups fish stock

1 fresh chili, seeded and chopped

salt and freshly ground black pepper

sprigs of fresh parsley, to garnish

3 Add the cod, fish stock, chili and seasoning and bring to a boil. Lower the heat and simmer for about 20 minutes, or until the cod is cooked through and flakes easily.

4 Peel the cooked bananas and cut into slices. Stir into the soup and heat through for a few minutes. Ladle into soup bowls and garnish with parsley. Serve.

1 Slit the skins of the green bananas and place in a large saucepan. Cover with water and bring to a boil over medium heat. Cook for 25 minutes until the bananas are tender. Transfer to a plate and leave to cool.

2 Melt the butter or margarine in a large saucepan. Add the onion and sauté for about 5 minutes until soft. Stir in the tomatoes and okra and fry slowly for 10 minutes longer.

Fish Ball Soup

The Japanese name for this soup is Tsumire-jiru. Tsumire *means, quite literally, sardine balls, and these are added to this delicious soup to impart their robust flavor.*

INGREDIENTS

Serves 4

7 tablespoons sake or dry white wine

5 cups instant dashi

4 tablespoons white miso paste

5 ounces shimeji mushrooms or
   6 shiitake mushrooms

1 leek or large scallion

For the fish balls

¾ ounce fresh ginger root

1¾ pounds fresh sardines, dressed and
   heads removed

2 tablespoons white miso paste

1 tablespoon sake or dry white wine

1½ teaspoons sugar

1 egg

2 tablespoons cornstarch

1 Make the fish balls: Grate the ginger and squeeze it well to yield 1 teaspoon ginger juice.

2 Rinse the sardines under cold water. Cut in half along the backbone and remove all the bones. To skin a boned sardine, lay it skin-side down on a board, then run a sharp knife slowly along the skin from tail to head.

3 Coarsely chop the sardines and process with the ginger juice, miso, sake or wine, sugar, and egg to make a thick paste in a food processor or blender. Transfer to a bowl and mix in the cornstarch until thoroughly blended.

4 If using shimeji mushrooms, trim the mushrooms then separate each stem. If using shiitake mushrooms, remove the stalks and shred them. Cut the leek or scallion into 1½-inch strips.

5 Bring the ingredients for the soup to a boil. Use 2 wet spoons to shape small portions of the sardine mixture into bite-size balls. Drop them into the soup and add the prepared mushrooms and leek or scallion.

6 Simmer the soup until the sardine balls float to the surface. Serve immediately, in deep soup bowls.

Chicken Minestrone

This is a special minestrone made with fresh chicken. Served with crusty Italian bread, it makes a hearty meal in itself.

INGREDIENTS

Serves 4 to 6

1 tablespoon olive oil

2 chicken thighs

3 bacon slices, chopped

1 onion, minced

a few fresh basil leaves, shredded

a few fresh rosemary leaves, minced

1 tablespoon chopped fresh flat-leaf
    parsley

2 potatoes, cut into ½-inch cubes

1 large carrot, cut into ½-inch cubes

2 small zucchini, cut into ½-inch cubes

1 or 2 celery stalks, cut into ½-inch cubes

1 quart chicken stock

1¾ cups frozen peas

scant 1 cup *stellette* or other small
    soup pasta

salt and freshly ground black pepper

Parmesan cheese shavings, to serve

1 Heat the oil in a large skillet. Add the chicken thighs and fry for about 5 minutes on each side; remove with a slotted spoon and set aside.

2 Add the bacon, onion, and herbs to the pan and cook slowly, stirring constantly, for about 5 minutes. Add the potatoes, carrot, zucchini, and celery and cook for 5 to 7 minutes longer.

3 Return the chicken thighs to the pan. Add the stock and bring to a boil. Cover and cook over low heat for 35 to 40 minutes, stirring the soup occasionally.

4 Remove the chicken thighs with a slotted spoon and place them on a board. Stir the peas and pasta into the soup and return to a boil. Simmer, stirring frequently, for 7 to 8 minutes or according to the directions on the package, until the pasta is just *al dente*.

5 Meanwhile, remove and discard the chicken skin. Remove the meat from the chicken bones and cut it into ½-inch pieces.

6 Return the meat to the soup, stir well, and heat through. Taste and adjust the seasoning as necessary.

7 Serve hot in warm soup bowls, topped with Parmesan shavings.

Pasta Squares and Peas in Broth

This thick soup is from Lazio, where it is traditionally made with fresh homemade pasta and peas. In this modern version, store-bought pasta is used with frozen peas to save time.

INGREDIENTS

Serves 4 to 6

2 tablespoons butter

$\frac{1}{3}$ cup roughly chopped pancetta or smoked bacon

1 small onion, minced

1 celery stalk, minced

3$\frac{1}{2}$ cups frozen peas

1 teaspoon tomato paste

1 to 2 teaspoons minced fresh flat-leaf parsley

1 quart chicken stock

11 ounces fresh lasagne noodles

about $\frac{1}{3}$ cup chopped Parma ham

salt and freshly ground black pepper

grated Parmesan cheese, to serve

1 Melt the butter in a large saucepan. Add the pancetta or bacon, onion, and celery and cook over low heat, stirring constantly, for 5 minutes.

COOK'S TIP

∽

Take care when adding salt because of the saltiness of the pancetta and the Parma ham.

2 Add the peas and cook, stirring, for 3 to 4 minutes. Stir in the tomato paste, parsley, stock, and salt and pepper to taste. Bring to a boil. Cover the pan, lower the heat, and simmer for 10 minutes. Meanwhile, cut the lasagne noodles into $\frac{3}{4}$-inch squares.

3 Taste the soup and adjust the seasoning. Drop in the pasta, stir, and bring to a boil. Simmer for 2 to 3 minutes, or until the pasta is *al dente*. Stir in the ham. Serve hot in warm bowls, with grated Parmesan handed around separately.

Squash, Bacon, and Swiss Cheese Soup

This is a lightly spiced squash soup, enriched with plenty of creamy melting cheese.

INGREDIENTS

Serves 4

2 pounds butternut squash

8 ounces smoked slab bacon

1 tablespoon oil

1½ cups roughly chopped onions

2 garlic cloves, crushed

2 teaspoons ground cumin

1 tablespoon ground coriander

2 cups diced potatoes

3¾ cups vegetable stock

2 teaspoons cornstarch

2 tablespoons sour cream

hot-pepper sauce, to taste

salt and freshly ground black pepper

1½ cups grated Gruyère cheese,
    to serve

crusty bread, to serve

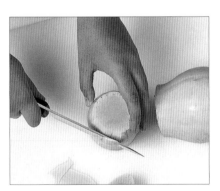

1 Cut the squash into large pieces. Using a sharp knife, carefully remove the skin, wasting as little flesh as possible.

2 Scoop out and discard the seeds. Chop the squash into small chunks. Remove all the fat from the bacon and roughly chop it into small pieces.

3 Heat the oil in a large saucepan. Add the onions and garlic and cook for 3 minutes, or until they begin to become soft.

4 Add the bacon and cook for about 3 minutes. Stir in the spices and cook over low heat for a minute longer.

5 Add the chopped squash, potatoes, and stock. Bring to a boil and simmer for 15 minutes, or until the squash and potatoes are tender.

6 Blend the cornstarch with 2 tablespoons water and add to the soup with the sour cream. Bring to a boil and simmer, uncovered, for 3 minutes. Adjust the seasoning and add hot-pepper sauce to taste.

7 Ladle the soup into warm bowls and sprinkle the cheese on top. Serve immediately with crusty bread to scoop up the melted cheese.

COOK'S TIP

Pumpkin can be used instead of butternut squash, and is equally delicious.

Split Pea and Ham Soup

The main ingredient for this dish is ham hock, which is the narrow piece of bone cut from a leg of ham. You could use a piece of belly of pork instead, if you prefer, and remove it with the herbs before serving.

INGREDIENTS

Serves 4

2½ cups green split peas

4 bacon slices

1 onion, roughly chopped

2 carrots, sliced

1 celery stalk, sliced

2½ quarts cold water

1 sprig of fresh thyme

2 bay leaves

1 large potato, roughly diced

1 ham hock

freshly ground black pepper

1 Put the split peas into a bowl, cover with cold water, and leave to soak overnight.

2 Cut the bacon into small pieces. In a large saucepan, dry-fry the bacon for 4 to 5 minutes or until crisp. Remove from the pan with a slotted spoon.

3 Add the onion, carrots, and celery to the fat in the pan and cook for 3 to 4 minutes until the onion is soft but not brown. Return the bacon to the pan with the water.

4 Drain the split peas and add to the pan with the thyme, bay leaves, potato, and ham hock and bring to a boil. Lower the heat, cover, and simmer for 1 hour.

5 Remove the thyme, bay leaves and hock. Process the soup in a blender or food processor until smooth. Return to the rinsed pan. Cut the meat from the hock, add to the soup and heat through gently. Season with plenty of freshly ground black pepper. Ladle into warm soup bowls and serve.

Lentil, Bacon and Frankfurter Soup

This is a wonderfully hearty German soup, but a lighter version can be made by omitting the frankfurters, if preferred.

INGREDIENTS

Serves 6

1 cup brown lentils
1 tablespoon sunflower oil
1 onion, finely chopped
1 leek, finely chopped
1 carrot, finely diced
2 celery stalks, chopped
4-ounce piece lean slab bacon
2 bay leaves
1½ quarts water
2 tablespoons chopped fresh parsley,
   plus extra to garnish
2 cups sliced frankfurters
salt and freshly ground black pepper

1 Rinse the lentils thoroughly under cold water; drain well.

2 Heat the oil in a large pan. Add the onion and slowly fry for 5 minutes until soft. Add the leek, carrot, celery, bacon, and bay leaves.

COOK'S TIP
~

Unlike most legumes, brown lentils do not need to be soaked before cooking.

3 Add the lentils. Pour in the water and slowly bring to a boil. Skim any foam from the surface. Simmer, half-covered, for 45 to 50 minutes, or until the lentils are soft.

4 Remove the piece of bacon from the soup and cut into small cubes. Trim off any fat.

5 Return the bacon to the soup with the parsley and sliced frankfurters, and season well with salt and freshly ground black pepper. Simmer for 2 to 3 minutes. Remove the bay leaves.

6 Transfer to soup bowls and garnish with chopped parsley. Serve hot.

Pork and Noodle Broth with Shrimp

This delicately flavored soup from Vietnam is quick and easy to make, while tasting really special. The noodles make the soup into a satisfying and wholesome dish.

INGREDIENTS

Serves 4 to 6

12 ounces pork chops or tenderloin

8 ounces raw or cooked shrimp

5 ounces thin egg noodles

1 tablespoon vegetable oil

2 teaspoons sesame oil

4 shallots or 1 onion, sliced

1 tablespoon finely sliced fresh
   ginger root

1 garlic clove, crushed

1 teaspoon sugar

1½ quarts chicken stock

2 kaffir lime leaves

3 tablespoons fish sauce

juice of ½ lime

For the garnish

4 sprigs of fresh cilantro

2 scallions, green parts only,
   chopped

1 If you are using pork chops rather than the tenderloin, remove any fat and the bones. Place the pork in the freezer for 30 minutes to firm, but do not freeze it: This makes it easier to slice thinly. Once sliced, set aside.

2 If using raw shrimp, peel and devein them.

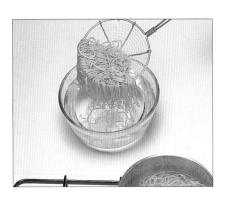

3 Bring a large saucepan of salted water to a boil. Add the egg noodles and cook according to the directions on the package. Drain and refresh under cold water; set the noodles to one side.

4 Heat a wok. Add the vegetable and sesame oils and heat through. When the oil is hot, add the shallots or onion and stir-fry for 3 to 4 minutes until evenly brown. Remove from the wok and set aside.

5 Add the ginger, garlic, sugar, and chicken stock to the wok and bring to a simmer. Add the lime leaves, fish sauce and lime juice. Add the pork, lower the heat, and simmer for 15 minutes.

6 Add the shrimp and noodles and simmer for 3 to 4 minutes, or longer if using raw shrimp to make sure that they cook through.

7 Serve garnished with the cilantro sprigs and the green parts of the scallions.

VARIATION

This quick-and-delicious recipe can be made with 7 ounces boneless chicken breast instead of pork fillets.

Three-Delicacy Soup

This delicious soup combines the three ingredients of chicken, ham, and shrimp.

INGREDIENTS

Serves 4

4 ounces boneless chicken breast meat

4 ounces honey-roasted ham

4 ounces shelled shrimp

3 cups chicken stock

salt

chopped scallions, to garnish

COOK'S TIP

Fresh, uncooked shrimp impart the best flavor. If these are not available, you can use cooked shrimp, but add them toward the end of cooking so they don't overcook.

1 Thinly slice the chicken breast and ham into small pieces. If the shrimp are large, cut them in half lengthwise.

2 In a wok or saucepan, bring the stock to a rolling boil. Add the chicken, ham, and shrimp and return to a boil. Add salt to taste and simmer for 1 minute.

3 Ladle into soup bowls. Serve hot, garnished with chopped scallions.

Lamb and Cucumber Soup

This is a very simple soup to prepare, but still tastes delicious.

INGREDIENTS

Serves 4

8 ounces boneless lamb steak

1 tablespoon light soy sauce

2 teaspoons Chinese rice wine or
    dry sherry

1/2 teaspoon sesame oil

3-inch piece cucumber

3 cups chicken or vegetable stock

1 tablespoon rice vinegar

salt and freshly ground white pepper

1 Trim off any excess fat from the lamb. Thinly slice the lamb into small pieces. Marinate in the soy sauce, wine or sherry, and sesame oil for 25 to 30 minutes. Discard the marinade.

2 Halve the cucumber piece lengthwise, but do not peel. Cut into thin slices diagonally.

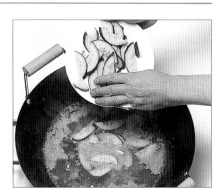

3 In a wok or saucepan, bring the stock to a rolling boil. Add the lamb and stir to separate.

4 Return to a boil. Add the cucumber, vinegar, and seasoning. Return to a boil and serve at once.

Bulgarian Sour Lamb Soup

This traditional sour soup is made with lamb, though pork and poultry are popular alternatives.

INGREDIENTS

Serves 4 to 5

2 tablespoons oil

1 pound lean boneless lamb, trimmed and cubed

1 onion, diced

2 tablespoons all-purpose flour

1 tablespoon paprika

1 quart lamb stock, hot

3 sprigs of fresh parsley

4 scallions

4 sprigs of fresh dill

scant ¼ cup long-grain rice

2 eggs, beaten

2 to 3 tablespoons vinegar or lemon juice, or more, to taste

salt and freshly ground black pepper

For the garnish

2 tablespoons butter

1 teaspoon paprika

a little fresh parsley or lovage and dill

1 In a large pan, heat the oil. Add the meat and fry until it is brown. Add the onion and cook until it is soft. Sprinkle in the flour and paprika. Stir well, add the stock, and cook for 10 minutes.

2 Tie the parsley, scallions and dill together and add to the pan with the rice and seasoning. Bring to a boil. Lower the heat and simmer for 30 to 40 minutes, or until the lamb is tender.

3 Remove the pan from the heat and stir in the eggs. Add the vinegar or lemon juice. Discard the tied herbs and season to taste.

4 To make the garnish, melt the butter in a pan and add the paprika. Ladle the soup into warm bowls. Garnish with the herbs and a little of the red paprika butter.

Meatball and Pasta Soup

*This soup, which comes from sunny
Sicily, is substantial enough to
make a hearty supper, whatever
the weather.*

INGREDIENTS

Serves 4

2 x 11-ounce cans condensed beef
    consommé

¾ cup very thin pasta, such as *fidelini*
    or *spaghettini*

chopped fresh flat-leaf parsley, to garnish

grated Parmesan cheese, to serve

For the meatballs

1 very thick slice white bread, crusts
    removed

2 tablespoons milk

8 ounces ground beef

1 garlic clove, crushed

2 tablespoons grated Parmesan cheese

2 to 3 tablespoons fresh flat-leaf parsley
    leaves, coarsely chopped

1 egg

a generous pinch of freshly grated nutmeg

salt and freshly ground black pepper

1 Make the meatballs: Break the
bread into a small bowl and
add the milk: Set aside to soak.
Meanwhile, put the ground beef,
garlic, Parmesan, parsley, and egg
in a large bowl. Grate the nutmeg
liberally over the top and add salt
and pepper to taste.

2 Squeeze the bread with your
hands to remove as much milk
as possible. Add the bread to the
meatball mixture and mix
everything together well with your
hands. Wash your hands, rinse
them under the cold tap, and form
the mixture into tiny balls about
the size of small marbles.

3 Tip both cans of consommé
into a large saucepan. Add
water as directed on the labels
and an extra can of water. Season
to taste, bring to a boil and add
the meatballs.

4 Break the pasta into small
pieces and add it to the soup.
Bring to a boil, stirring gently.
Lower the heat, simmer, stirring
frequently, for 7 to 8 minutes or
according to the directions on the
package, until the pasta is *al dente*.
Taste and adjust the seasoning.

5 Ladle into warm bowls and
garnish with chopped parsley
and freshly grated Parmesan
cheese. Serve at once.

Clear Soup with Meatballs

A Chinese-style soup, in which meatballs are combined with lightly cooked vegetables in a flavorsome broth.

INGREDIENTS

Serves 8

4 to 6 dried Chinese mushrooms, soaked
   in warm water for 30 minutes
2 tablespoons peanut oil
1 large onion, minced
2 garlic cloves, minced
½-inch piece fresh ginger root, bruised
2¼ quarts beef or chicken stock,
   including the soaking liquid from
   the mushrooms
2 tablespoons soy sauce
1½ ounces shredded kale, spinach, or
   Napa cabbage

For the meatballs
6 ounces finely ground beef
1 small onion, minced
1 or 2 garlic cloves, crushed
1 tablespoon cornstarch
a little egg white, lightly beaten
salt and freshly ground black pepper

1 Prepare the meatballs: Mix the beef with the onion, garlic, cornstarch, and seasoning in a food processor. Bind the mixture with sufficient egg white to make it firm. With wet hands, roll into tiny, bite-size balls; set aside.

2 Drain the mushrooms, reserving the soaking liquid. Trim off and discard the stems. Slice the caps finely; set aside.

3 Heat a wok or large saucepan. Heat the oil. Add the onion, garlic, and ginger and fry to bring out the flavors, but do not let them brown.

4 When the onion is soft, pour in the stock and bring to a boil. Stir in the soy sauce and mushroom slices and simmer for 10 minutes. Add the meatballs and cook for 10 minutes.

5 Just before serving, remove the ginger. Stir in the shredded kale, spinach, or Napa cabbage. Heat through for 1 minute only —no longer or the leaves will be overcooked. Serve the soup at once.

Pork and Vegetable Soup

The unusual ingredients in this interesting Japanese soup are available from specialist food stores.

Serves 4

2 ounces gobo, optional

1 teaspoon rice vinegar

½ black konnyaku, about 4 ounces

2 teaspoons oil

7 ounces belly of pork, cut into thin
   1¼ to ½ inch long strips

1 cup peeled and thinly sliced daikon

½ cup thinly sliced carrot

1 potato, thinly sliced

4 shiitake mushrooms, stems removed
   and thinly sliced

3½ cups kombu and bonito stock or
   instant dashi, prepared

1 tablespoon sake or dry white wine

3 tablespoons red or white miso paste

For the garnish

2 scallions, thinly sliced

seven-spice flavor (*shichimi*)

1 Scrub the skin off the gobo, if using, with a vegetable brush. Slice the vegetable into fine shavings. Soak the prepared gobo for 5 minutes in plenty of water with the vinegar added to remove any bitter taste; drain.

2 Put the piece of konnyaku in a small pan and add enough water just to cover it. Bring to a boil over medium heat. Drain and leave to cool: This removes any bitter taste.

3 Using your hands, tear the konnyaku into ¾-inch lumps: Do not use a knife because a smooth cut surface will not absorb any flavor.

4 Heat the oil in a saucepan. Add the pork and stir-fry. Add the gobo, daikon, carrot, potato, shiitake mushrooms, and konnyaku and stir-fry for 1 minute. Pour in the stock and sake or wine.

5 Bring the soup to a boil, skim the surface and simmer for 10 minutes until the vegetables are soft.

6 Ladle a little of the soup into a small bowl and dissolve the miso paste in it. Pour the mixture back into the saucepan and return to a boil. Do not continue to boil or the flavor will be lost. Remove from the heat amd pour into individual bowls. Sprinkle with the scallions and seven-spice flavor (*shichimi*). Serve at once.

Tomato and Beef Soup

Fresh tomatoes and scallions give this light beef broth a superb flavor.

Serves 4

3 ounces sirloin steak, trimmed of fat

3¾ cups beef stock

2 tablespoons tomato paste

6 tomatoes, halved, seeded, and chopped

2 teaspoons sugar

1 tablespoon cornstarch

1 tablespoon cold water

1 egg white

½ teaspoon sesame oil

2 scallions, finely shredded

salt and freshly ground black pepper

3 Mix the cornstarch to a paste with the cold water. Add the paste to the soup, stirring constantly until it thickens slightly but does not become lumpy. Lightly beat the egg white in a cup.

4 Pour the egg white into the soup in a steady stream, stirring all the time. As soon as the egg white changes color, add salt and pepper, and stir the soup. Pour it into warm bowls. Drizzle a few drops of sesame oil on each portion and sprinkle with the scallions. Serve at once.

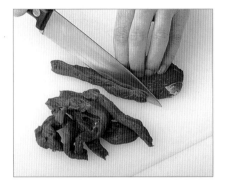

1 Cut the beef into thin strips and place it in a saucepan. Pour boiling water over to cover and cook for 2 minutes. Drain thoroughly; set aside.

2 Bring the stock to a boil in a clean pan. Stir in the tomato paste, the tomatoes, and the sugar. Add the beef, and return the stock to a boil. Lower the heat and simmer for 2 minutes.

Beef Chili Soup

This is a hearty dish based on a traditional chili recipe. It is ideal served with fresh, crusty bread as a warming start to any meal.

INGREDIENTS

Serves 4

1 tablespoon oil
1 onion, chopped
6 ounces ground beef
2 garlic cloves, chopped
1 fresh red chili, sliced
¼ cup all-purpose flour
14-ounce can crushed tomatoes
2½ cups beef stock
1⅓ cups canned kidney beans, drained
2 tablespoons chopped fresh parsley
salt and freshly ground black pepper
crusty bread, to serve

1 Heat the oil in a large saucepan. Add the onion and ground beef and fry for 5 minutes until brown and sealed.

2 Add the garlic, chili, and flour and cook for 1 minute. Add the tomatoes and pour in the stock. Bring to a boil.

3 Stir in the kidney beans and add salt and pepper to taste. Continue cooking for 20 minutes.

4 Add the parsley, reserving a little to garnish the finished dish. Pour the soup into warm bowls and sprinkle with the reserved parsley. Serve with crusty bread.

COOK'S TIP

For a milder flavor, remove the seeds from the chili after slicing.

ONE-POT-MEAL
SOUPS

Tuscan Bean Soup

V

There are many versions of this wonderful soup. This one uses cannellini beans, leeks, cabbage, and good olive oil—and tastes even better when it is reheated.

INGREDIENTS

Serves 4

3 tablespoons extra-virgin olive oil

1 onion, roughly chopped

2 leeks, roughly chopped

1 large potato, diced

2 garlic cloves, minced

1¼ cups vegetable stock

14-ounce can cannellini beans, drained and liquid reserved

generous 2 cups shredded Savoy cabbage

3 tablespoons chopped fresh flat-leaf parsley

2 tablespoons chopped fresh oregano

¾ cup shaved Parmesan cheese

salt and freshly ground black pepper

For the garlic toasts

2 to 3 tablespoons extra-virgin olive oil

6 thick slices country bread

1 garlic clove, peeled and bruised

1 Heat the oil in a large saucepan. Add the onion, leeks, potato, and garlic and cook slowly for 4 to 5 minutes until they begin to become soft.

2 Pour in the stock and the liquid from the beans. Cover and simmer for 15 minutes.

3 Stir in the beans, cabbage, and half the herbs. Season and cook for 10 minutes longer. Spoon about one-third of the soup into a food processor or blender and process until fairly smooth. Return to the soup in the pan and adjust the seasoning. Heat through for 5 minutes.

4 Make the garlic toasts: Drizzle a little oil over the slices of bread and rub both sides of each slice with the garlic. Broil until brown on both sides. Ladle the soup into bowls. Sprinkle with the remaining herbs and the Parmesan shavings. Add a drizzle of olive oil and serve with the hot garlic toasts.

Farmhouse Soup

Root vegetables form the basis of this chunky, minestrone-style main-course soup. Vary the vegetables according to what you have to hand.

INGREDIENTS

Serves 4

2 tablespoons olive oil

1 onion, roughly chopped

3 carrots, cut into large chunks

1½ cups turnips cut into large chunks

about 1½ cups rutabaga cut into
　large chunks

14-ounce can crushed Italian tomatoes

1 tablespoon tomato paste

1 teaspoon Italian seasoning

1 teaspoon dried oregano

½ cup dried peppers, finely sliced
　(optional)

1½ quarts vegetable stock or water

½ cup small macaroni or *conchiglie*

14-ounce can red kidney beans, rinsed
　and drained

2 tablespoons chopped fresh flat-leaf
　parsley

salt and freshly ground black pepper

grated Parmesan cheese, to serve

1 Heat the oil in a large saucepan. Add the onion and cook over low heat for about 5 minutes until soft. Add the fresh vegetables, canned tomatoes, tomato paste, Italian seasoning, and dried peppers, if using. Stir in salt and pepper to taste.

2 Pour in the stock or water and bring to a boil. Stir well, cover, lower the heat, and simmer for 30 minutes, stirring occasionally.

3 Add the pasta and return to a boil, stirring. Lower the heat and simmer, uncovered, for about 5 minutes, or according to the directions on the package until the pasta is just *al dente*. Stir frequently during the cooking.

4 Stir in the beans and heat through for 2 to 3 minutes. Remove from the heat and stir in the parsley. Taste and adjust the seasoning. Serve hot in warm soup bowls and hand around the grated Parmesan separately.

COOK'S TIP

Packages of dried Italian peppers are sold in many supermarkets and in delicatessens. They are piquant and firm with a "meaty" bite, which makes them ideal for adding substance to vegetarian soups.

V

Provençal Vegetable Soup

This satisfying soup captures all the flavors of summer in Provence. Pistou, the basil and garlic purée, gives it extra color and a wonderful aroma—so don't leave it out.

INGREDIENTS

Serves 6 to 8

1½ cups shelled fresh fava beans, or
 ¾ cup dried haricot beans, soaked
 overnight

½ teaspoon dried *herbes de Provence*

2 garlic cloves, minced

1 tablespoon olive oil

1 onion, minced

1 large leek, finely sliced

1 celery stalk, finely sliced

2 carrots, finely diced

2 small potatoes, finely diced

4 ounces thin green beans

1¼ quarts water

2 small zucchini, finely diced

3 tomatoes, peeled, seeded, and finely
 diced

1 cup shelled fresh or frozen peas

a handful of spinach leaves, cut into
 thin ribbons

salt and freshly ground black pepper

sprigs of fresh basil, to garnish

For the pistou

1 or 2 garlic cloves, minced

½ cup (packed) basil leaves

4 tablespoons grated Parmesan cheese

4 tablespoons extra-virgin olive oil

1 To make the pistou, put the garlic, basil, and Parmesan cheese in a food processor and process until smooth, scraping down the sides once. With the machine running, slowly add the olive oil through the feed tube. Alternatively, pound the garlic, basil, and cheese in a mortar and pestle and stir in the oil.

2 To make the soup, if using dried haricot beans, drain. Place them in a saucepan and cover with water. Boil vigorously for 10 minutes and drain.

3 Place the parboiled beans, or fresh beans, if using, in a saucepan with the *herbes de Provence* and one of the garlic cloves. Add water to cover by 1 inch and bring to a boil. Lower the heat and simmer over medium-low heat until tender, about 10 minutes for fresh beans or 1 hour for dried beans; set aside in the cooking liquid.

4 Heat the oil in a large saucepan or flameproof casserole. Add the onion and leek and cook for 5 minutes, stirring occasionally, until they are beginning to soften.

5 Add the celery, carrots, and the remaining garlic clove and cook, covered, for 10 minutes, stirring occasionally.

6 Add the potatoes, green beans, and water. Season lightly with salt and pepper and bring to a boil, skimming any foam from the surface. Lower the heat, cover, and simmer for 10 minutes.

7 Add the zucchini, tomatoes and peas, together with the reserved beans and their cooking liquid, and simmer for 25 to 30 minutes longer until all the vegetables are tender. Add the spinach and simmer for 5 minutes. Season the soup and swirl a spoonful of pistou into each bowl. Garnish with basil and serve.

COOK'S TIP
~

Both the pistou and the soup can be made 1 or 2 days in advance and chilled. To serve, reheat slowly, stirring occasionally.

[V]

Chunky Bean and Vegetable Soup

A substantial soup, not unlike minestrone, using a selection of vegetables, with cannellini beans for extra protein and fiber. Serve with a hunk of wholegrain bread.

INGREDIENTS

Serves 4

2 tablespoons olive oil

2 celery stalks, chopped

2 leeks, sliced

3 carrots, sliced

2 garlic cloves, crushed

14-ounce can crushed tomatoes with basil

1¼ quarts vegetable stock

14-ounce can cannellini beans (or mixed legumes), drained

1 tablespoon pesto sauce

salt and freshly ground black pepper

Parmesan cheese shavings, to serve

1 Heat the olive oil in a large saucepan. Add the celery, leeks, carrots, and garlic and cook slowly for about 5 minutes until they are soft.

2 Stir in the tomatoes and stock and bring to a boil. Lower the heat, cover, and simmer for 15 minutes.

3 Stir in the beans and pesto, with salt and pepper to taste. Heat through for 5 minutes longer. Serve in warm bowls, sprinkled with shavings of Parmesan cheese.

COOK'S TIP

Extra vegetables can be added to the soup to make it even more substantial. For example, add thinly sliced zucchini or finely shredded cabbage for the last 5 minutes of the cooking time. Or, stir in some small whole-wheat pasta shapes, if liked. Add them at the same time as the tomatoes, as they will take 10 to 15 minutes to cook.

Caribbean Vegetable Soup

V

This vegetable soup is refreshing and filling, and a good choice for a main lunch dish.

INGREDIENTS

Serves 4

2 tablespoons butter or margarine

1 onion, chopped

1 garlic clove, crushed

2 carrots, sliced

1½ quarts vegetable stock

2 bay leaves

2 sprigs of fresh thyme

1 celery stalk, minced

2 green bananas, peeled and cut into 4 pieces

1¼ cups peeled and cubed white yam or eddoe

2 tablespoons red lentils

1 chayote, peeled and chopped

2 tablespoons macaroni (optional)

salt and freshly ground black pepper

chopped scallions, to garnish

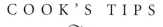

COOK'S TIPS

Use other root vegetables or potatoes if yam or eddoes are not available. Add more stock if you want a thinner soup.

1 Melt the butter or margarine. Add the onion, garlic, and carrots and fry for a few minutes, stirring occasionally, until they begin to soften. Add the stock, bay leaves, and thyme and bring to a boil.

2 Add the celery, green bananas, white yam or eddoe, lentils, chayote and macaroni, if using. Season and simmer for 25 minutes, or until all the vegetables are cooked. Serve garnished with chopped scallions.

Chunky Pasta Soup

V

Serve this hearty, main-meal soup with tasty, pesto-topped French bread croutons.

INGREDIENTS

Serves 4

½ cup dried beans (a mixture of red kidney and haricot beans), soaked overnight

1¼ quarts water

1 tablespoon oil

1 onion, chopped

2 celery stalks, finely sliced

2 or 3 garlic cloves, crushed

2 leeks, finely sliced

1 vegetable bouillon cube

14-ounce can or jar pimientos

3 to 4 tablespoons tomato paste

1 cup pasta shapes

4 slices French bread

1 tablespoon pesto sauce

l cup baby corn cobs, halved

½ cup each broccoli and cauliflower flowerets

a few drops of hot-pepper sauce

salt and freshly ground black pepper

1 Place the beans in a large pan with the water. Bring to a boil, lower the heat and simmer for about 1 hour, or until almost tender.

2 When the beans are almost ready, heat the oil in a large pan and fry the vegetables for 2 minutes. Add the bouillon cube and the beans with about 2½ cups of their liquid. Cover and simmer for 10 minutes.

3 Meanwhile, purée the pimientos with a little of their liquid and add to the pan. Stir in the tomato paste and pasta and cook for 15 minutes. Heat the oven to 400°F.

4 Meanwhile, make the pesto croutons. Spread the French bread with the pesto sauce and bake for 10 minutes, or until crisp.

5 When the pasta is just cooked, add the corn, broccoli and cauliflower flowerets, hot-pepper sauce, and seasoning to taste. Heat through for 2 to 3 minutes. Serve at once with the pesto croutons.

Japanese Crushed Tofu Soup

V

Look in Japanese food stores or health-food stores for burdock root. Konnyaku is sold in small rectangular slabs or fresh in tubs of water.

INGREDIENTS

Serves 4

5 ounces fresh firm tofu, weighed
   without water

2 dried shiitake mushrooms

2 ounces *gobo*

1 teaspoon rice vinegar

4 ounces black or white konnyaku

2 tablespoons sesame oil

¾ cup finely sliced daikon

½ cup finely sliced carrots

3 cups kombu and bonito stock or
   instant dashi

a pinch of salt

2 tablespoons sake or dry white wine

1½ teaspoons mirin

3 tablespoons white or red miso paste

a dash of soy sauce

6 snow peas, trimmed, boiled and finely
   sliced, to garnish

1 Crush the tofu coarsely by hand until it resembles lumpy scrambled egg in texture—do not crush it too finely.

2 Wrap the tofu in a clean dish towel and put it in a strainer. Pour over plenty of boiling water and leave the tofu to drain thoroughly for 10 minutes.

3 Soak the dried shiitake mushrooms in tepid water for 20 minutes, then drain them. Remove their stems and cut the caps into 4 to 6 pieces.

4 Use a vegetable brush to scrub the skin off the burdock root and slice it into thin shavings. Soak the shavings for 5 minutes in plenty of cold water with the vinegar added to remove any bitter taste; drain.

5 Put the konnyaku in a small saucepan and cover with water. Bring to a boil; drain and leave to cool. Tear the konnyaku into ¾-inch lumps: Do not use a knife, because smooth cuts will prevent it from absorbing flavor.

6 Heat the sesame oil in a deep saucepan. Add all the shiitake mushrooms, burdock root, daikon, carrots, and konnyaku and stir-fry for 1 minute. Add the tofu and stir well.

7 Pour in the stock or dashi and add the salt, sake or wine, and mirin. Bring to a boil. Skim the broth and simmer it for 5 minutes.

8 In a small bowl, dissolve the miso paste in a little of the soup, then return it to the pan. Simmer the soup for 10 minutes until the vegetables are soft. Add the soy sauce, then remove from the heat. Serve immediately in 4 bowls, garnished with the snow peas.

V

Genoese Minestrone

In Genoa, they often make minestrone like this, with pesto stirred in toward the end of cooking. It is packed full of vegetables and has a strong, heady flavor, making it an excellent vegetarian supper dish when served with bread. There is Parmesan cheese in the pesto, so there is no need to serve any extra with the soup.

INGREDIENTS

Serves 4 to 6

3 tablespoons olive oil

1 onion, minced

2 celery stalks, minced

1 large carrot, minced

5 ounces thin green beans, cut into 2-inch pieces

1 zucchini, finely sliced

1 potato, cut into ½-inch cubes

¼ Savoy cabbage, shredded

1 small eggplant, cut into ½-inch cubes

7-ounce can cannellini beans, drained and rinsed

2 Italian plum tomatoes, chopped

1¼ quarts vegetable stock

3½ ounces spaghetti or vermicelli

salt and freshly ground black pepper

For the pesto

about 20 fresh basil leaves

1 garlic clove

2 teaspoons pine nuts

1 tablespoon freshly grated Parmesan cheese

1 tablespoon freshly grated Pecorino cheese

2 tablespoons olive oil

1 Heat the oil in a large saucepan. Add the onion, celery, and carrot and cook over low heat, stirring frequently, for 5 to 7 minutes.

2 Stir in the green beans, zucchini, potato, and Savoy cabbage and stir-fry over medium heat for about 3 minutes. Add the eggplant, cannellini beans, and plum tomatoes and stir-fry for 2 to 3 minutes longer.

3 Pour in the stock with salt and pepper to taste and bring to a boil. Stir well, cover, lower the heat and simmer for 40 minutes, stirring occasionally.

4 Meanwhile, process all the pesto ingredients in a food processor until the mixture forms a smooth sauce, adding 1 to 3 tablespoons water through the feeder tube if the sauce seems too thick.

5 Break the pasta into small pieces and add it to the soup. Simmer, stirring frequently, for 5 minutes. Stir in the pesto sauce and simmer for 2 to 3 minutes longer, or until the pasta is *al dente*. Check the seasoning and serve hot, in warm soup bowls.

Summer Minestrone

This brightly colored, fresh-tasting soup makes the most of delicious summer vegetables.

INGREDIENTS

Serves 4

3 tablespoons olive oil

1 large onion, minced

1 tablespoon sun-dried tomato paste

3 cups peeled and chopped ripe Italian plum tomatoes

1½ cups trimmed and roughly chopped zucchini

1½ cups trimmed and roughly chopped yellow zucchini

3 waxy new potatoes, diced

2 garlic cloves, crushed

about 1¼ quarts vegetable stock or water

4 tablespoons shredded fresh basil

⅔ cup grated Parmesan cheese

salt and freshly ground black pepper

1 Heat the oil in a large saucepan. Add the onion and cook slowly for about 5 minutes, stirring constantly, until soft.

2 Stir in the sun-dried tomato paste, chopped tomatoes, zucchini, diced potatoes, and garlic and cook slowly for 10 minutes, uncovered, shaking the pan frequently to stop the vegetables from sticking to the base.

3 Pour in the stock or water and bring to a boil. Lower the heat, half-cover the pan, and simmer for 15 minutes, or until the vegetables are just tender. Add more stock if necessary.

4 Remove the pan from the heat and stir in the basil and half the cheese. Taste and adjust the seasoning. Serve hot, sprinkled with the remaining cheese.

Seafood Laksa

For a delicious meal, serve creamy rice noodles in a spicy coconut-flavored soup, topped with seafood. Compressed shrimp paste, called blachan, is sold in Oriental food stores.

INGREDIENTS

Serves 4

4 fresh red chilies, seeded and roughly chopped

1 onion, roughly chopped

1 piece shrimp paste, the size of a stock cube

1 lemongrass stalk, chopped

1 small piece fresh ginger root, peeled and roughly chopped

6 macadamia nuts or almonds

4 tablespoons vegetable oil

1 teaspoon paprika

1 teaspoon ground turmeric

2 cups fish stock

2½ cups coconut milk

a dash of fish sauce, to taste

12 jumbo shrimp, shelled and deveined

8 scallops

8 ounces prepared squid, cut into rings

12 ounces rice vermicelli or rice noodles, soaked in warm water until soft

salt and freshly ground black pepper

lime halves, to serve

For the garnish

¼ cucumber, cut into matchsticks

2 fresh red chilies, seeded and finely sliced

2 tablespoons mint leaves

2 tablespoons fried shallots or onions

1 In a blender or food processor, process the chilies, onion, shrimp paste, lemongrass, ginger, and nuts until smooth.

2 Heat 3 tablespoons of the oil in a large saucepan. Add the chili paste and fry for 6 minutes. Stir in the paprika and turmeric and fry for about 2 minutes longer.

3 Add the stock and the coconut milk to the pan and bring to a boil. Lower the heat and simmer for 15 to 20 minutes. Season with fish sauce.

4 Season the seafood with salt and pepper. Stir-fry in the remaining oil for 2 to 3 minutes until cooked.

5 Add the noodles to the soup and heat through. Divide between individual bowls. Place the fried seafood on top and garnish with the cucumber, chilies, mint, and fried shallots or onions. Serve at once with the limes for squeezing over each portion.

Clam and Pasta Soup

This soup is a variation of the pasta dish spaghetti alla vongole, *using pantry ingredients. Serve it with warm focaccia or ciabatta for an informal supper with friends.*

INGREDIENTS

Serves 4

2 tablespoons olive oil

1 large onion, minced

2 garlic cloves, crushed

14-ounce can crushed tomatoes

1 tablespoon sun-dried tomato paste

1 teaspoon sugar

1 teaspoon Italian seasoning

about 3 cups fish or vegetable stock

²/₃ cup red wine

¹/₂ cup small pasta shapes

5-ounce jar or can clams in natural juice

2 tablespoons finely chopped fresh flat-leaf parsley, plus a few whole leaves to garnish

salt and freshly ground black pepper

1 Heat the oil in a large saucepan. Add the onion and cook for 5 minutes, stirring frequently, until soft.

2 Add the garlic, tomatoes, tomato paste, sugar, seasoning, stock, wine, and salt and pepper to taste and bring to a boil. Lower the heat, half-cover the pan, and simmer for 10 minutes, stirring occasionally.

3 Add the pasta and continue simmering, uncovered, for about 10 minutes, or until *al dente*, stirring occasionally to prevent the pasta shapes from sticking together.

4 Add the clams and their juice to the soup and heat through for 3 to 4 minutes, adding more stock if required: Do not allow it to boil or the clams will become tough. Remove from the heat, stir in the chopped parsley and adjust the seasoning. Serve hot, sprinkled with coarsely ground black pepper and parsley leaves.

Shrimp Creole

Raw shrimp are combined with chopped fresh vegetables and cayenne pepper to make this tasty soup.

INGREDIENTS

Serves 4

1½ pounds raw shrimp in the shells, with heads, if available

2 cups water

3 tablespoons olive or vegetable oil

1½ cups minced onions

½ cup minced celery

½ cup minced green pepper

½ cup chopped fresh parsley

1 garlic clove, crushed

1 tablespoon Worcestershire sauce

¼ teaspoon cayenne pepper

½ cup dry white wine

½ cup chopped peeled plum tomatoes

1 teaspoon salt

1 bay leaf

1 teaspoon sugar

fresh parsley, to garnish

boiled rice, to serve

1 Shell and devein the shrimp, reserving the heads and shells. Keep the shrimp in a covered bowl in the refrigerator while you make the sauce.

2 Put the shrimp heads and shells in a pan with the water and bring to a boil. Lower the heat and simmer for 15 minutes. Strain and reserve 1½ cups of the stock.

3 Heat the oil in a heavy saucepan. Add the onions and cook over low heat for 8 to 10 minutes until soft. Add the celery and green pepper and cook for 5 minutes longer. Stir in the parsley, garlic, Worcestershire sauce, and cayenne and continue cooking for another 5 minutes.

4 Raise the heat to medium. Stir in the wine and simmer for 3 to 4 minutes. Add the tomatoes, reserved shrimp stock, salt, bay leaf, and sugar and bring to a boil. Stir well, lower the heat to low, and simmer for about 30 minutes until the tomatoes fall apart and the sauce reduces slightly. Remove from the heat and leave to cool slightly.

5 Discard the bay leaf. Pour the soup into a food processor or blender and purée until smooth. Taste and adjust the seasoning as necessary.

6 Return the tomato purée to the pan and bring to a boil. Lower the heat, add the shrimp and simmer for 4 to 5 minutes until they turn pink. Ladle into soup bowls and garnish with fresh parsley. Serve with rice.

Creamy Fish Chowder

A traditional soup that never fails to please, whether it is made with milk or, more luxuriously, with a generous quantity of cream.

INGREDIENTS

Serves 4

3 thick-cut slab bacon slices

1 large onion, minced

1½ pounds potatoes, diced

1 quart fish stock

1 pound skinless haddock, cut into 1-inch cubes

2 tablespoons chopped fresh parsley

1 tablespoon snipped fresh chives

1¼ cups whipping cream or whole milk

salt and freshly ground black pepper

1 Remove any rind from the bacon and discard it. Cut the bacon into small pieces. Chop the onion and cut the potatoes into ¾-inch cubes.

2 Fry the bacon in a deep saucepan until the fat is rendered. Add the onion and potatoes and cook over a low heat, without browning, for about 10 minutes. Season to taste .

3 Pour off excess bacon fat from the pan. Add the fish stock to the pan and bring to a boil. Simmer 15 to 20 minutes until the vegetables are tender.

4 Stir in the cubes of fish, the parsley and chives. Simmer 3 to 4 minutes, or until the fish is just cooked.

5 Stir the cream or milk into the chowder and reheat slowly. Do not bring to a boil. Season to taste and serve at once.

VARIATION

∽

Cod fillets are equally good in this chowder. Or, use smoked fillets for a stronger flavor.

Bouillabaisse

Perhaps the most famous of all Mediterranean fish soups, this recipe, originating from Marseilles, is a rich and colorful mixture of fish and shellfish, flavored with tomatoes, saffron, orange, and a splash of anise-flavored liquor.

INGREDIENTS

Serves 4 to 6

3½ pounds mixed fish and raw shellfish, such as mullet, John Dory, monkfish, red snapper, whiting, jumbo raw shrimp, and clams

8 ounces well-flavored tomatoes

a pinch of saffron strands

6 tablespoons olive oil

1 onion, sliced

1 leek, sliced

1 celery stalk, sliced

2 garlic cloves, crushed

1 bouquet garni

1 strip orange peel

½ teaspoon fennel seeds

1 tablespoon tomato paste

2 teaspoons Pernod or other anise-flavored liquor

salt and freshly ground black pepper

4 to 6 thick slices French bread and 3 tablespoons chopped fresh parsley, to serve

---

COOK'S TIP

Saffron comes from the orange and red stigmas of a specific type of crocus, which are harvested by hand and are, therefore, very expensive— the highest-priced spice in the world. Its flavor, however, is unique and cannot be replaced by any other spice. It is an essential ingredient in traditional bouillabaisse and should not be omitted.

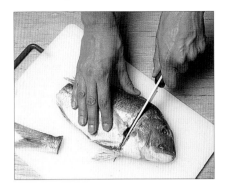

1 Remove the heads, tails, and fins from the fish and set the fish aside. Put the trimmings in a large pan with 1¼ quarts water and bring to a boil. Simmer for 15 minutes, strain and reserve the liquid.

2 Cut the fish into large chunks. Leave the shellfish in their shells. Scald the tomatoes. Drain and refresh them in cold water, then peel them and chop roughly. Soak the saffron in 1 to 2 tablespoons hot water.

3 Heat the oil in a large pan. Add the onion, leek, and celery and cook until soft. Add the garlic, bouquet garni, orange peel, fennel seeds, and chopped tomatoes. Stir in the saffron and its soaking liquid and the reserved fish stock. Season with salt and pepper and bring to a boil. Lower the heat and simmer for 30 to 40 minutes.

4 Add the shellfish and boil for about 6 minutes. Add the fish and cook for 6 to 8 minutes longer, until it flakes easily.

5 Using a slotted spoon, transfer the fish to a warmed serving platter. Keep the liquid boiling, so the oil emulsifies with the broth. Add the tomato paste and liquor, and check the seasoning to taste.

6 Ladle into warm bowls and scatter with chopped parsley. Serve with French bread.

Provençal Fish Soup with Pasta

This colorful soup captures all the flavors of the Mediterranean. Serve it as a main course for a deliciously filling lunch.

INGREDIENTS

Serves 4

2 tablespoons olive oil

1 onion, sliced

1 garlic clove, crushed

1 leek, sliced

1 quart water

8 ounces canned crushed tomatoes

a pinch of Mediterranean herbs

$1/4$ teaspoon saffron strands (optional)

1 cup small pasta

about 8 live mussels in the shell

1 pound white fish, such as cod, flounder, or monkfish, filleted and skinned

salt and freshly ground black pepper

For the rouille

2 garlic cloves, crushed

1 canned pimiento, drained and chopped

1 tablespoon fresh white bread crumbs

4 tablespoons mayonnaise

toasted French bread, to serve

1 Heat the oil in a large saucepan. Add the onion, garlic, and leek, cover and cook slowly for 5 minutes, stirring occasionally, until the vegetables are soft.

2 Add the water, tomatoes, herbs, saffron, if using, and pasta. Season and cook for 15 to 20 minutes.

3 Scrub the mussels and pull off the "beards." Discard any that do not close when sharply tapped.

4 Cut the fish into bite-size chunks and add to the soup, placing the mussels on top. Simmer for 5 to 10 minutes until the mussels open and the fish is cooked. Discard any unopened mussels.

5 To make the *rouille*, pound together the garlic, canned pimiento, and bread crumbs in a mortar and pestle, or use a blender or food processor. Stir in the mayonnaise and season well.

6 Spread the toasted French bread with the rouille and serve with the soup.

Fisherman's Soup

There is something delicious about the combined flavors of bacon and fish.

INGREDIENTS

Serves 4

6 slices bacon, cut into strips

1 tablespoon butter

1 large onion, chopped

1 garlic clove, minced

2 tablespoons chopped fresh parsley

1 teaspoon fresh thyme leaves or
  ½ teaspoon dried thyme

3 cups peeled, seeded, and
  chopped tomatoes

⅔ cup dry vermouth or white wine

2 cups fish stock

2 cups diced potatoes

1½ to 2 pounds skinless white fish fillets,
  cut into large chunks

salt and freshly ground black pepper

fresh flat-leaf parsley, to garnish

1 Dry-fry the bacon in a large saucepan over medium heat until light brown, but not crisp. Remove from the pan and drain on paper towels.

2 Melt the butter in the pan. Add the onion and cook, stirring occasionally, for 3 to 5 minutes until soft. Add the garlic and herbs and continue cooking for 1 minute, stirring. Add the tomatoes, vermouth or wine, and stock and bring to a boil.

3 Lower the heat, cover, and simmer the stew for 15 minutes. Add the potatoes, cover again, and simmer for 10 to 12 minutes longer or until the potatoes are almost tender.

COOK'S TIP

In winter, when fresh tomatoes are lacking in flavor, substitute canned crushed tomatoes. The soup will taste slightly different, but will still be successful.

4 Add the chunks of fish and the bacon strips. Simmer, uncovered, for 5 minutes, or until the fish is just cooked and the potatoes are tender. Adjust the seasoning and garnish with flat-leaf parsley; serve at once.

Corn Chowder with Conchigliette

Corn kernels combine with smoked turkey and pasta to make this satisfying and filling one-pot meal, perfect for a hungry family or for guests.

INGREDIENTS

Serves 6 to 8

1 small green bell pepper

1 pound diced potatoes

2 cups canned or frozen corn kernels

1 onion, chopped

1 celery stalk, chopped

1 bouquet garni

2½ cups chicken stock

1¼ cups skim milk

½ cup *conchigliette*

oil, for frying

5 ounces diced smoked turkey

salt and freshly ground black pepper

breadsticks, to serve

3 Add the milk and salt and pepper. Process half of the soup in a food processor or blender and return to the pan with the pasta. Simmer for 10 minutes, or until the pasta is *al dente*.

4 Heat the oil in a nonstick skillet. Add the turkey and fry quickly for 2 to 3 minutes. Stir into the soup. Serve the soup with breadsticks.

1 Seed the green pepper and cut it into dice. Cover with boiling water and leave to stand for 2 minutes: Drain and rinse.

2 Put the potatoes into a saucepan with the corn, onion, celery, diced pepper, bouquet garni, and stock and bring to a boil. Lower the heat, cover, and simmer for 20 minutes, or until all the ingredients are tender.

Thai Chicken and Noodle Soup

This makes full use of the characteristic Thai flavors of garlic, coconut, lemon, peanut butter, fresh cilantro, and chili.

INGREDIENTS

Serves 4

1 tablespoon vegetable oil

1 garlic clove, minced

2 skinless, boneless chicken breasts, halved, about 6 ounces each, chopped

$\frac{1}{2}$ teaspoon turmeric

$\frac{1}{4}$ teaspoon cayenne pepper

$\frac{1}{2}$ cup grated creamed coconut

$3\frac{3}{4}$ cups chicken stock, hot

2 tablespoons lemon or lime juice

2 tablespoons crunchy peanut butter

1 cup thread egg noodles broken into small pieces

1 tablespoon chopped scallions

1 tablespoon chopped fresh cilantro

salt and freshly ground black pepper

shredded coconut and finely chopped fresh red chili, to garnish

1 Heat the oil in a large pan. Add the garlic and fry for 1 minute until light golden. Add the chicken and spices and stir-fry for 3 to 4 minutes.

2 Sprinkle the creamed coconut into the hot chicken stock and stir until it dissolves. Pour onto the chicken meat and add the lemon or lime juice, peanut butter, and thread egg noodles.

3 Cover the pan and simmer for 15 minutes. Add the scallions and fresh cilantro, season well with salt and freshly ground black pepper. Simmer for 5 minutes longer.

4 Meanwhile, heat the shredded coconut and chili in a small, dry skillet for 2 to 3 minutes, stirring frequently, until the coconut is light brown.

5 Pour the soup into bowls and sprinkle with the dry-fried coconut and chili. Serve at once.

Chicken, Tomato, and Chayote Soup

Chayote, also known by its French name christophene, *is a gourd-like fruit with a central seed. It is a popular ingredient in Latin American cuisines.*

INGREDIENTS

Serves 4

1½ cups skinless, boneless chicken
   breast meat
1 garlic clove, crushed
a pinch of freshly grated nutmeg
2 tablespoons butter or margarine
½ onion, minced
1 tablespoon tomato paste
14-ounce can tomatoes, puréed
1¼ quarts chicken stock
1 fresh chili, seeded and chopped
2½ cups peeled and diced chayote
1 teaspoon dried oregano
½ teaspoon dried thyme
⅓ cup skinned and diced smoked
   haddock fillet
salt and freshly ground black pepper
snipped fresh chives, to garnish

1 Dice the chicken. Place it in a bowl and season with salt, pepper, garlic, and nutmeg. Stir well to flavor; set aside for about 30 minutes.

2 Melt the butter or margarine in a large saucepan. Add the chicken and sauté over medium heat for 5 to 6 minutes. Stir in the onion and fry slowly for 5 minutes longer, or until the onion is slightly soft.

3 Add the tomato paste, puréed tomatoes, stock, chili, chayote, and herbs and bring to a boil. Cover and simmer for 35 minutes, or until the chayote is tender.

4 Add the smoked fish and simmer for 5 minutes longer, or until the fish is cooked through. Adjust the seasoning and pour into warm soup bowls and garnish with a scattering of snipped fresh chives. Serve piping hot.

Chunky Chicken Soup

This thick chicken and vegetable soup is served with garlic-flavored fried croutons.

INGREDIENTS

Serves 4

4 skinless, boneless chicken thighs

1 tablespoon butter

2 small leeks, thinly sliced

2 tablespoons long-grain rice

3¾ cups chicken stock

1 tablespoon chopped mixed fresh parsley and mint

salt and freshly ground black pepper

For the garlic croutons

2 tablespoons olive oil

1 garlic clove, crushed

4 slices bread, cut into cubes

1 Cut the chicken into ½-inch cubes. Melt the butter in a saucepan. Add the leeks and cook until tender. Add the rice and chicken and cook for 2 minutes.

2 Add the stock. Cover the pan and simmer for 15 to 20 minutes until the rice is tender.

3 To make the garlic croutons, heat the oil in a large skillet. Add the crushed garlic clove and bread cubes and cook until the bread is golden brown, stirring all the time to prevent burning. Drain on paper towels and sprinkle with a pinch of salt.

4 Add the parsley and mint to the soup and adjust the seasoning to taste. Serve with the garlic croutons.

Noodles in Soup

In China, noodles in soup (tang mein) are far more popular than fried noodles (chow mein). You can adapt this basic recipe by using different ingredients for the "dressing."

INGREDIENTS

Serves 4

8 ounces chicken breast meat, pork
 tenderloin or any cooked meat

3 or 4 shiitake mushrooms, soaked

4 ounces canned sliced bamboo shoots,
 drained

4 ounces spinach leaves, lettuce hearts,
 or Napa cabbage leaves

2 scallions

12 ounces dried egg noodles

2½ cups stock

2 tablespoons vegetable oil

1 teaspoon salt

½ teaspoon light brown sugar

1 tablespoon light soy sauce

2 teaspoons Chinese rice wine or
 dry sherry

a few drops of sesame oil

hot red-chili sauce, to serve

1 Thinly shred the meat. Squeeze dry the shiitake mushrooms and discard any hard stems. Thinly shred the mushrooms, bamboo shoots, greens, and scallions.

2 Cook the noodles in boiling water according to the directions on the package. Drain and rinse under cold water. Place in a serving bowl.

3 Bring the stock to a boil and pour over the noodles; set aside and keep warm.

4 Heat the oil in a hot wok. Add about half of the scallions and the meat and stir-fry for about 1 minute.

5 Add the mushrooms, bamboo shoots, and greens and stir-fry for 1 minute. Add the salt, sugar, soy sauce, and rice wine or sherry and blend well.

6 Pour the "dressing" over the noodles, garnish with the remaining scallions, and sprinkle a few drops of sesame oil over. Divide into soup bowls and serve with hot red-chili sauce.

Chiang Mai Noodle Soup

A signature dish of the city of Chiang Mai, this delicious noodle soup has Burmese origins and is the Thai equivalent of the Malaysian dish laksa.

INGREDIENTS

Serves 4 to 6

2½ cups coconut milk

2 tablespoons red curry paste

1 teaspoon ground turmeric

3 cups chicken thigh meat cut into
  bite-size chunks

2½ cups chicken stock

4 tablespoons fish sauce

1 tablespoon dark soy sauce

juice of ½ to 1 lime

1 pound fresh egg noodles, blanched
  briefly in boiling water

salt and freshly ground black pepper

For the garnish

3 scallions, chopped

4 fresh red chilies, chopped

4 shallots, chopped

4 tablespoons sliced pickled mustard
  leaves, rinsed

2 tablespoons fried sliced garlic

fresh cilantro leaves

4 fried noodle nests (optional)

1 Pour about one-third of the coconut milk into a large saucepan and bring to a boil, stirring often with a wooden spoon until it separates.

2 Add the curry paste and turmeric, stir to mix together, and cook until fragrant.

3 Add the chicken and stir-fry for about 2 minutes, ensuring all the chunks are coated with the paste.

4 Add the remaining coconut milk, chicken stock, fish sauce, and soy sauce. Season to taste and simmer for 7 to 10 minutes. Remove from the heat and stir in the lime juice.

5 Reheat the noodles in boiling water; drain and divide between individual bowls. Divide the chicken between the bowls and ladle in the hot soup. Top each serving of soup with a few of each of the garnishes.

Chicken Soup with Vermicelli

In Morocco, the cook—who is almost always the most senior female of the household—will use a whole chicken for this nourishing soup, to serve to her large extended family. This is a slightly simplified version, using chicken portions.

INGREDIENTS

Serves 4 to 6

2 tablespoons sunflower oil

1 tablespoon butter

1 onion, chopped

2 chicken legs or breast, halved
    or quartered

flour for dusting

2 carrots, cut into 1½-inch pieces

1 parsnip, cut into 1½-inch pieces

1½ quarts chicken stock

1 cinnamon stick

a good pinch of paprika

a pinch of saffron

2 egg yolks

juice of ½ lemon

2 tablespoons chopped fresh cilantro

2 tablespoons chopped fresh parsley

5 ounces vermicelli

salt and freshly ground black pepper

1 Heat the oil and butter in a saucepan or flameproof casserole. Add the onion and fry for 3 to 4 minutes until soft. Dust the chicken pieces in seasoned flour and fry slowly until they are evenly browned.

2 Transfer the chicken to a plate and add the carrots and parsnip to the pan. Cook over low heat for 3 to 4 minutes, stirring frequently. Return the chicken to the pan and add the stock, cinnamon stick, and paprika. Season well with salt and pepper.

3 Bring the soup to a boil. Cover and simmer for 1 hour until the vegetables are very tender.

4 Meanwhile, blend the saffron in 2 tablespoons boiling water. Beat the egg yolks with the lemon juice in a separate bowl and add the cilantro and parsley. When the saffron water has cooled, stir into the egg and lemon mixture.

5 When the vegetables are tender, transfer the chicken to a plate. Spoon off any excess fat from the soup. Increase the heat a little and stir in the noodles. Cook for 5 to 6 minutes until the noodles are tender. Meanwhile, remove the skin and bones from the chicken and chop the meat into bite-size pieces.

6 When the vermicelli is cooked stir in the chicken pieces and the egg, lemon, and saffron mixture. Cook over low heat for 1 to 2 minutes, stirring all the time. Adjust the seasoning and serve.

Mulligatawny Soup

Mulligatawny *(which literally means "pepper water") was introduced into England in the late eighteenth century by members of the colonial services returning home from India.*

INGREDIENTS

Serves 4

4 tablespoons butter, or 4 tablespoons oil

2 large chicken joints, about 12 ounces each

1 onion, chopped

1 carrot, chopped

1 small turnip, chopped

about 1 tablespoon curry powder, to taste

4 cloves

6 black peppercorns, lightly crushed

¼ cup lentils

3¾ cups chicken stock

¼ cup golden raisins

salt and freshly ground black pepper

1 Melt the butter or heat the oil in a large saucepan. Add the chicken and brown over a brisk heat. Transfer the chicken to a plate; set aside.

2 Add the onion, carrot, and turnip to the pan and cook, stirring occasionally, until lightly colored. Stir in the curry powder, cloves, and crushed peppercorns and cook for 1 to 2 minutes. Add the lentils.

3 Pour the stock into the pan and bring to a boil. Add the golden raisins, the chicken, and any juices from the plate. Cover and simmer for about 1¼ hours.

COOK'S TIP

❧

Choose red split lentils for the best color, although either green or brown lentils can also be used.

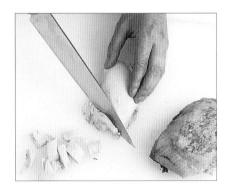

4 Remove the chicken from the pan and discard the skin and bones. Chop the meat, return to the soup, and reheat. Check the seasoning before serving the soup piping hot.

Smoked Turkey and Lentil Soup

Lentils enhance the flavor of smoked turkey, and combined with four tasty vegetables they make a fine meal-in-a-pot.

INGREDIENTS

Serves 4

2 tablespoons butter

1 large carrot, chopped

1 onion, chopped

1 leek, white part only, chopped

1 celery stalk, chopped

1½ cups chopped mushrooms

¼ cup dry white wine

1¼ quarts chicken stock

2 teaspoons dried thyme

1 bay leaf

½ cup lentils

¾ cup diced smoked turkey meat

salt and freshly ground black pepper

1 Melt the butter in a large saucepan. Add the carrot, onion, leek, celery, and mushrooms and cook for 3 to 5 minutes until golden.

2 Stir in the wine and chicken stock and bring to a boil. Skim off any foam from the surface. Add the thyme and bay leaf. Lower the heat, cover, and simmer for 30 minutes.

3 Add the lentils and continue cooking, covered, for 30 to 40 minutes longer until they are just tender. Stir the soup occasionally.

4 Add the turkey and season to taste with salt and pepper. Cook until just heated through. Ladle into bowls and serve.

Cock-a-Leekie

This traditional Scottish recipe—it is known from as long ago as 1598 —originally included beef as well as chicken. In the olden days, it would have been made from an old cock bird, hence the name.

INGREDIENTS

Serves 4

2 chicken portions, about 10 ounces each

1¼ quarts chicken stock

1 bouquet garni

4 leeks

8 to 12 prunes, soaked

salt and freshly ground black pepper

bread, to serve

1 Put the chicken portions into a saucepan with the stock and bouquet garni and bring to a boil. Simmer gently for 40 minutes.

2 Cut the white part of the leeks into 1-inch slices and finely slice a little of the green part.

3 Add the white part of the leeks and the prunes to the saucepan and cook slowly for 20 minutes. Add the green part of the leeks and cook for 10 to 15 minutes longer.

4 Remove the bouquet garni and discard. Take the chicken out of the pan, discard the skin and bones, and chop the meat. Return the chopped meat to the pan and season the soup.

5 Heat the soup through slowly. Ladle into warm soup bowls and serve hot with bread.

Scotch Broth

Sustaining and warming, Scotch Broth makes a delicious one-pot meal anytime.

INGREDIENTS

Serves 6

2 pounds lean neck of lamb, cut into large, even-size chunks

1¾ quarts water

1 large onion, chopped

¼ cup pearl barley

1 bouquet garni

1 large carrot, chopped

1 turnip, chopped

3 leeks, chopped

½ small white cabbage, shredded

salt and freshly ground black pepper

chopped fresh parsley, to garnish
 (optional)

1 Put the lamb and water into a large saucepan and bring to a boil. Skim off the foam. Stir in the onion, barley, and bouquet garni.

2 Bring the soup back to a boil. Partly cover the saucepan and simmer for 1 hour. Add the remaining vegetables and the seasoning and return to a boil. Partly cover again and simmer for about 35 minutes until the vegetables are tender.

3 Remove surplus fat from the top of the soup. Serve the soup hot, sprinkled with chopped parsley, if liked.

Lamb, Bean, and Pumpkin Soup

This is a hearty soup to warm the cockles of the heart in even the chilliest weather.

INGREDIENTS

Serves 4

²/₃ cup split black-eyed peas, soaked for
    1 to 2 hours or overnight

1½ pounds neck of lamb, cut into
    medium-size chunks

1 teaspoon chopped fresh thyme, or
    ½ teaspoon dried thyme

2 bay leaves

1¼ quarts stock or water

1 onion, sliced

8 ounces diced pumpkin

2 black cardamom pods

1½ teaspoons turmeric

1 tablespoon chopped fresh cilantro

½ teaspoon caraway seeds

1 fresh green chili, seeded and chopped

2 green bananas

1 carrot

salt and freshly ground black pepper

1 Drain the black-eyed peas, place them in a saucepan, and cover with fresh cold water.

2 Bring the beans to a boil and boil rapidly for 10 minutes. Lower the heat and simmer, covered, for 40 to 50 minutes until tender, adding more water if necessary. Remove the pan from the heat; set aside to cool.

3 Meanwhile, put the lamb in a large saucepan. Add the thyme, bay leaves, and stock or water and bring to a boil. Cover and simmer over medium heat for 1 hour until tender.

4 Stir in the onion, pumpkin, cardamoms, turmeric, cilantro, caraway, chili and seasoning. Return to a simmer and cook, uncovered, for 15 minutes, stirring occasionally, until the pumpkin is tender.

5 When the beans are cool, spoon them into a blender or food processor with their liquid and blend to a smooth purée.

6 Peel the bananas and cut into medium slices. Cut the carrot into thin slices. Stir into the soup with the bean purée and cook for 10 to 12 minutes, until the carrot is tender. Adjust the seasoning and serve.

Lamb and Lentil Soup

Lamb and lentils go together so well they almost seem to have been made for one another.

Serves 4

About 1½ quarts water or stock

2 pounds neck of lamb, cut into chops

½ onion, chopped

1 garlic clove, crushed

1 bay leaf

1 clove

2 sprigs of fresh thyme

1½ cups potatoes cut into
   1-inch pieces

¾ cup red lentils

salt and freshly ground black pepper

chopped fresh parsley

1 Put about 1¼ quarts of the stock or water and the meat in a large saucepan with the onion, garlic, bay leaf, clove, and sprigs of thyme and bring to a boil. Simmer for about 1 hour until the lamb is tender.

COOK'S TIP
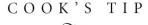

Red lentils do not need soaking before they are cooked; simply pick them over and remove any pieces of grit, and rinse well.

2 Add the potato pieces and the lentils to the pan and season the soup with a little salt and plenty of black pepper. Add the remaining stock or water to come just above the surface of the meat and vegetables; you may need more if the soup becomes too thick during cooking.

3 Cover and allow to simmer for 25 minutes, or until the lentils are cooked and well blended into the soup. Taste the soup and adjust the seasoning as necessary. Stir in the parsley and serve.

Moroccan Harira

This substantial meat and vegetable soup is traditionally eaten during the month of Ramadan, when the Moroccan Muslim population fasts between sunrise and sunset.

INGREDIENTS

Serves 4

2 tablespoons butter

8 ounces lamb, cut into ½-inch pieces

1 onion, chopped

1 pound well-flavored tomatoes

4 tablespoons chopped fresh cilantro

2 tablespoons chopped fresh parsley

½ teaspoon turmeric

½ teaspoon ground cinnamon

¼ cup red lentils

½ cup chick-peas, soaked overnight

2½ cups water

4 pearl onions or small shallots, peeled

¼ cup soup noodles

salt and freshly ground black pepper

For the garnish

chopped fresh cilantro

lemon slices

ground cinnamon

2 Peel the tomatoes, if you wish, by plunging them into boiling water to loosen the skins. Wait for them to cool a little before peeling. Cut them into quarters and add to the lamb with the herbs and spices.

3 Rinse the lentils under cold running water and drain the chick-peas. Add both to the pan with the water. Season with salt and pepper and bring to a boil. Cover and simmer for 1½ hours.

4 Add the baby onions or small shallots and simmer for 30 minutes longer. Add the noodles 5 minutes before the end of the cooking time. Serve the soup when the noodles are tender, garnished with the cilantro, lemon slices, and cinnamon.

1 Heat the butter in a large saucepan or flameproof casserole. Add the lamb and onion and fry for 5 minutes, stirring frequently.

Spinach and Lemon Soup with Meatballs

This soup, known as aarshe saak, *is almost standard fare in many parts of the Middle East. In Greece, it is made without the meatballs and is simply called* avgolemono.

INGREDIENTS

Serves 6

2 large onions

3 tablespoons oil

1 tablespoon turmeric

½ cup yellow split peas

1¼ quarts water

8 ounces ground lamb

6 cups chopped spinach

½ cup rice flour

juice of 2 lemons

1 or 2 garlic cloves, minced

2 tablespoons chopped fresh mint

4 eggs, beaten

salt and freshly ground black pepper

sprigs of fresh mint, to garnish

1 Chop one of the onions and fry in 2 tablespoons of the oil in a large pan until golden. Add the turmeric, peas, and water and bring to a boil. Simmer for 20 minutes.

2 Grate the other onion into a bowl, add the lamb and seasoning and stir. Using your hands, form the mixture into small balls, about the size of walnuts. Carefully add to the pan and simmer for 10 minutes. Add the spinach, cover, and simmer for 20 minutes longer.

3 Mix the flour with about 1 cup cold water to make a smooth paste. Slowly add to the pan, stirring all the time. Add the lemon juice, season and cook over low heat for 20 minutes.

4 Meanwhile, heat the remaining oil in a small pan. Add the garlic and fry quickly until golden. Stir in the mint and remove the pan from the heat.

5 Remove the soup from the heat and stir in the beaten eggs. Sprinkle the prepared garlic and mint mixture over the soup and garnish with mint sprigs. Serve at once.

Bean and Pasta Soup

This hearty, main-meal soup sometimes goes by the simpler name of pasta e fagioli, *while some Italians refer to it as* minestrone di pasta e fagioli. *Traditional recipes use dried beans and a ham bone.*

INGREDIENTS

Serves 4 to 6

2 tablespoons olive oil

⅔ cup diced pancetta or rindless
   smoked bacon

1 onion

1 carrot

1 celery stalk

1¾ cups beef stock

1 cinnamon stick or a good pinch of
   ground cinnamon

scant 1 cup small pasta shapes, such as
   conchiglie or *coralini*

14-ounce can borlotti beans, rinsed
   and drained

1½ cups diced cooked ham

salt and freshly ground black pepper

Parmesan cheese shavings, to serve

1 Heat the oil in a large saucepan. Add the pancetta or bacon and cook, stirring, until lightly colored. Finely chop the vegetables, add to the pan and cook for about 10 minutes, stirring frequently, until lightly colored. Pour in the stock, add the cinnamon with salt and pepper to taste, and bring to a boil. Lower the heat, cover, and simmer for 15 to 20 minutes.

2 Add the pasta shapes. Return to a boil, stirring all the time. Lower the heat and simmer, stirring frequently, for 5 minutes. Add the borlotti beans and diced ham and simmer for 2 to 3 minutes, or according to the directions on the package, until the pasta is *al dente*.

3 Remove the cinnamon stick, if used, taste the soup, and adjust the seasoning. Serve hot in warm bowls, sprinkled with Parmesan shavings.

VARIATION

If you prefer, use spaghetti or tagliatelle instead of the small pasta shapes, breaking it into small pieces over the pan. Use cannellini or white haricot beans instead of the borlotti. Add them to the pan after the stock in step 1. If you like, add 1 tablespoon tomato paste along with the beans.

Bacon and Lentil Soup

Serve this hearty soup with chunks of warm, crusty bread.

INGREDIENTS

Serves 4

3½ cups diced slab bacon

1 onion, roughly chopped

1 small turnip, roughly chopped

1 celery stalk, chopped

1 potato, roughly chopped

1 carrot, sliced

½ cup lentils

1 bouquet garni

freshly ground black pepper

fresh flat-leaf parsley, to garnish

1 Heat a large pan and add the bacon. Cook for a few minutes, allowing the fat to run out.

2 Add the chopped onion, turnip, celery, potato, and carrot. Cook for 4 minutes, stirring from time to time.

3 Add the lentils, bouquet garni, seasoning, and enough water to cover and bring to a boil. Simmer for 1 hour, or until the lentils are tender. Pour the soup into warm bowls and serve garnished with flat-leaf parsley.

Noodle Soup with Pork and Szechuan Pickle

This soup is a meal in itself and the hot pickle gives it a delicious tang.

INGREDIENTS

Serves 4

1 quart chicken stock

12 ounces egg noodles

1 tablespoon dried shrimp, soaked in water

2 tablespoons vegetable oil

1¾ cups finely shredded lean pork

1 tablespoon yellow bean paste

1 tablespoon soy sauce

4 ounces Szechuan hot pickle, rinsed, drained, and shredded

a pinch of sugar

2 scallions, finely sliced, to garnish

1 Bring the stock to a boil in a large saucepan. Add the noodles and cook until almost tender. Drain the noodles and reserve the stock. Lower the heat and simmer for 2 minutes longer; keep hot.

2 Heat the oil in a frying pan or wok. Add the pork and stir-fry over high heat for 3 minutes.

3 Add the bean paste and soy sauce to the pork and stir-fry for 1 minute. Add the hot pickle with a pinch of sugar and stir-fry for 1 minute longer.

4 Divide the noodles and soup between individual bowls. Spoon the pork mixture on top and sprinkle with the scallions. Serve at once.

Galician Broth

This delicious main-meal soup is very similar to the warming, chunky meat and potato broths of cooler climates. For extra color, a few onion skins can be added when cooking the ham, but remember to remove them before serving.

INGREDIENTS

Serves 4

1-pound piece gammon

2 bay leaves

2 onions, sliced

1½ quarts cold water

2 teaspoons paprika

1½ pounds potatoes, cut into large chunks

8 ounces collard greens

14-ounce can haricot or cannellini beans, drained

salt and freshly ground black pepper

1 Soak the ham overnight in cold water. Drain and put in a large saucepan with the bay leaves and onions and pour the water on top.

2 Bring to a boil. Lower the heat and simmer for about 1½ hours until the meat is tender: Keep an eye on the pan to make sure it doesn't boil over.

COOK'S TIP

Ham knuckles can be used instead of the ham. The bones will give the juices a delicious flavor.

3 Drain the meat, reserving the cooking liquid, and leave to cool slightly. Discard the skin and any excess fat from the meat. Cut the meat into small chunks. Return to the pan with the cooking liquid, paprika and potatoes. Cover and simmer for 20 minutes.

4 Remove the cores from the greens. Roll up the leaves and cut into thin shreds. Add to the pan with the beans and simmer for about 10 minutes. Season with salt and freshly ground black pepper to taste. Serve piping hot.

Seafood and Sausage Gumbo

Gumbo is a soup, but it is often served over rice as a main course.

Serves 10 to 12

3 pounds raw shrimp in shell

1½ quarts water

4 onions, 2 of them quartered

4 bay leaves

¾ cup vegetable oil

1 cup all-purpose flour

5 tablespoons margarine or butter

2 green bell peppers, seeded and minced

4 celery stalks, minced

1½ pounds Polish or andouille sausage, cut into ½-inch slices

3 cups fresh okra, cut into ½-inch slices

3 garlic cloves, crushed

½ teaspoon fresh or dried thyme leaves

2 teaspoon salt

½ teaspoon freshly ground black pepper

½ teaspoon white pepper

1 teaspoon cayenne pepper

2 tablespoons hot pepper sauce (optional)

2 cups chopped, peeled fresh or canned plum tomatoes

1 pound fresh crabmeat

boiled rice, to serve

1 Peel and devein the shrimp; reserve the heads and shells. Cover and chill the shrimp while you make the sauce.

2 Place the shrimp heads and shells in a saucepan with the water, quartered onion, and 1 of the bay leaves and bring to a boil. Partly cover and simmer for 20 minutes. Strain and set aside.

3 To make a Cajun roux, heat the oil in a heavy-bottomed skillet. When the oil is hot, add the flour, a little at a time, and blend to a smooth paste.

4 Cook over medium-low heat, stirring constantly for 25 to 40 minutes until the roux reaches the color of peanut butter. Remove the pan from the heat and continue stirring until the roux cools and stops cooking.

5 Melt the margarine or butter in a large, heavy-bottomed saucepan or flameproof casserole. Finely chop the remaining onions and add to the pan with the peppers and celery. Cook over medium-low heat for 6 to 8 minutes, until the onions are soft, stirring occasionally.

6 Add the sausage, stir well, and cook for 5 minutes longer. Add the okra and garlic, stir, and cook until the okra stops producing white "threads."

7 Add the remaining bay leaves, the thyme, salt, black and white pepper, cayenne pepper, and hot-pepper sauce to taste, if using. Stir well then stir in 1½ quarts of the shrimp stock and the plum tomatoes. Bring to a boil, partly cover the pan, lower the heat, and simmer for about 20 minutes.

8 Whisk in the Cajun roux. Raise the heat and bring to a boil, whisking well. Lower the heat again and simmer, uncovered, for 40 to 45 minutes longer, stirring occasionally.

9 Stir in the shrimp and crabmeat. Cook for at least 3 to 4 minutes or until the shrimp turn pink.

10 To serve, put a mound of hot, boiled rice in each serving bowl and ladle the gumbo over, making sure each person gets some prawns, some crabmeat, and some sausage.

Green Herb Gumbo

Traditionally served at the end of Lent, this is a joyful, sweetly spiced and revitalizing dish, even if you haven't been fasting. The variety of green ingredients is important, so buy substitutes if you cannot find all of them.

INGREDIENTS

Serves 6 to 8

12-ounce piece raw smoked ham
2 tablespoons lard or vegetable oil
1 large Spanish onion, roughly chopped
2 or 3 garlic cloves, crushed
1 teaspoon dried oregano
1 teaspoon dried thyme
2 bay leaves
2 cloves
2 celery stalks, finely sliced
1 green bell pepper, seeded and chopped
1/2 green cabbage, stalk removed and
    finely shredded
2 1/4 quarts light stock or water
3 cups finely shredded spring greens
    or kale
3 cups finely shredded Chinese
    mustard cabbage
3 cups shredded spinach
1 bunch of watercress, shredded
6 scallions, finely shredded
1/2 cup chopped fresh parsley
1/2 teaspoon ground allspice
1/4 nutmeg, grated
a pinch of cayenne pepper
salt and freshly ground black pepper
warm French or garlic bread, to serve

1 Dice the ham very small, keeping any fat and rind in one separate piece. Put the fat with the lard or oil into a deep saucepan and heat until it sizzles. Stir in the diced ham, onion, garlic, oregano, and thyme and cook over medium heat for 5 minutes, stirring occasionally.

2 Add the bay leaves, cloves, celery, and green pepper and stir over medium heat for another 2 to 3 minutes. Add the cabbage and stock or water and bring to a boil. Lower the heat and simmer for 5 minutes.

3 Add the spring greens or kale and mustard cabbage and boil for 2 minutes longer. Add the spinach, watercress, and scallions and return to a boil. Lower the heat and simmer for 1 minute. Add the parsley, allspice, nutmeg, salt, black pepper, and cayenne to taste.

4 Remove the piece of ham fat and, if you can find them, the cloves. Ladle into soup bowls and serve at once, with warm French bread or garlic bread.

Beef and Herb Soup with Yogurt

This classic Iranian soup, aashe maste, *is a meal in itself and is a popular cold-weather dish.*

INGREDIENTS

Serves 4

2 large onions

2 tablespoons oil

1 tablespoon turmeric

½ cup yellow split peas

1¼ quarts water

8 ounces ground beef

1 cup long-grain rice

3 tablespoons each chopped fresh parsley, cilantro, and chives

1 tablespoon butter

1 large garlic clove, minced

4 tablespoons chopped fresh mint

2 or 3 saffron strands dissolved in
   1 tablespoon boiling water (optional)

salt and freshly ground black pepper

fresh mint, to garnish

plain yogurt and naan bread, to serve

1 Chop one of the onions. Heat the oil in a large saucepan. Add the chopped onion and fry until golden brown. Add the turmeric, split peas, and water and bring to a boil. Lower the heat and simmer for 20 minutes.

2 Grate the other onion into a bowl. Add the ground beef and seasoning and mix well. Using your hands, form the mixture into small balls about the size of walnuts. Carefully add to the pan and simmer for 10 minutes.

3 Add the rice, parsley, cilantro, and chives. Simmer for about 30 minutes until the rice is tender, stirring frequently.

4 Melt the butter in a small pan. Add the garlic and gently fry. Stir in the mint and sprinkle over the soup with the saffron, if using.

5 Spoon the soup into warm bowls. Garnish with mint and serve with yogurt and naan bread.

COOK'S TIP

Fresh spinach is also delicious in this soup. Add ½ cup finely chopped spinach leaves along with the parsley, cilantro, and chives.

Beef Noodle Soup

Offer your fortunate friends or family a steaming bowl of this soup, packed with delicious flavors of the Orient.

Serves 4

¼ ounce dried porcini mushrooms

⅔ cup boiling water

6 scallions

4 ounces carrots

12 ounces sirloin steak

about 2 tablespoons oil

1 garlic clove, crushed

1-inch piece fresh ginger root, peeled
   and minced

1¼ quarts beef stock

3 tablespoons light soy sauce

4 tablespoons dry sherry

3 ounces thin egg noodles

1 cup shredded spinach

salt and freshly ground black pepper

1 Break the mushrooms into small pieces. Place in a bowl and pour the boiling water over, and leave to soak for 15 minutes.

2 Shred the scallions and carrots into 2-inch long, fine strips. Trim any fat off the meat and slice into thin strips.

3 Heat the oil in a large saucepan. Add the beef in batches and cook until brown, adding a little more oil if necessary. Remove the beef with a slotted spoon and drain on paper towels.

4 Add the garlic, ginger, scallions and carrots to the pan and stir-fry for 3 minutes.

5 Add the beef, beef stock, the mushrooms and their soaking liquid, soy sauce, and sherry. Season generously with salt and freshly ground black pepper and bring to a boil. Lower the heat and simmer, covered, for 10 minutes.

6 Break up the noodles and add to the pan with the shredded spinach. Simmer for 5 minutes, until the beef is tender. Adjust the seasoning to taste before serving.

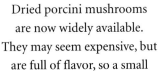

COOK'S TIP

Dried porcini mushrooms are now widely available. They may seem expensive, but are full of flavor, so a small quantity goes a long way and really gives a lift to a soup like this one.

Vegetable Broth with Ground Beef

This is a veritable cornucopia of flavors, combining to produce a rich and satisfying broth.

INGREDIENTS

Serves 6

2 tablespoons peanut oil

4 ounces finely ground beef

1 large onion, grated or minced

1 garlic clove, crushed

1 or 2 fresh chilies, seeded and chopped

½-inch cube shrimp paste, prepared

3 macadamia nuts or 6 almonds, finely
  ground

1 carrot, finely grated

1 teaspoon brown sugar

1 quart chicken stock

2 ounces dried shrimp, soaked in warm
  water for 10 minutes

3 cups finely shredded spinach

8 baby corn, sliced cobs, or 1⅓ cups
  canned whole-kernel corn

1 large tomato, chopped

juice of ½ lemon

salt

1 Heat the oil in a saucepan. Add the beef, onion, and garlic and cook, stirring, until the meat changes color.

2 Add the chilies, shrimp paste, macadamia nuts or almonds, carrot, sugar, and salt to taste.

3 Add the stock and bring slowly to a boil. Lower the heat to a simmer and then add the soaked shrimp, with their soaking liquid. Simmer for about 10 minutes.

4 A few minutes before serving, add the spinach, corn, tomato, and lemon juice. Simmer for 1 to 2 minutes to heat through: Do not overcook at this stage because this will spoil both the appearance and the taste of the end result. Serve at once.

COOK'S TIP

To make this broth very hot and spicy, add the seeds from the chilies.

Beef Broth with Cassava

This "big" soup is almost like a stew. The addition of wine is not traditional, but enhances the richness of the broth.

Serves 4

1 pound stewing beef, cubed

1¼ quarts beef stock

1¼ cups white wine

1 tablespoon soft brown sugar

1 onion, minced

1 bay leaf

1 bouquet garni

1 sprig of fresh thyme

1 tablespoon tomato paste

1 large carrot, sliced

2 cups cubed cassava or yam

⅔ cup chopped spinach

a little hot-pepper sauce, to taste

salt and freshly ground black pepper

2 Add the carrot, cassava or yam, spinach, a few drops of hot-pepper sauce and salt and pepper, and simmer for 15 minutes longer until both the meat and vegetables are tender. Serve.

COOK'S TIP

If you like, a cheap cut of lamb can be used instead of beef, and any other root vegetable can be used instead of, or as well as, the cassava or yam. Noodles, pasta shapes, or macaroni can also be used as a base, in which case reduce the amount of root vegetables. You can, if you prefer, omit the wine and add more water.

1 Put the beef, stock, wine, sugar, onion, bay leaf, bouquet garni, thyme, and tomato paste in a large saucepan and bring to a boil. Lower the heat, cover, and simmer for about 1¼ hours.

 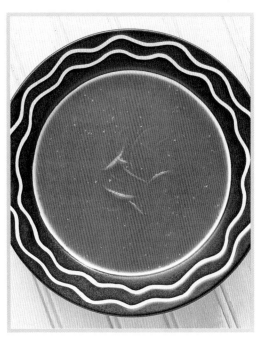 

SPECIAL
OCCASION
SOUPS

V

Melon and Basil Soup

This is a deliciously refreshing, chilled fruit soup, just right for a hot summer's day.

Serves 4 to 6

2 Charentais or canteloupe melons

scant ½ cup sugar

¾ cup water

finely grated peel and juice of 1 lime

3 tablespoons shredded fresh basil, plus
   whole leaves, to garnish

1 Cut the melons in half across the middle. Scrape out the seeds and discard. Using a melon baller, scoop out 20 to 24 balls; set aside for the garnish. Scoop out the remaining flesh and place in a blender or food processor.

COOK'S TIP

Add the syrup in two stages, because the amount of sugar needed will depend on the sweetness of the melon.

2 Place the sugar, water, and lime peel in a small pan over low heat. Stir until dissolved and bring to a boil. Lower the heat and simmer for 2 to 3 minutes. Remove from the heat and leave to cool slightly. Pour half the mixture into the blender or food processor with the melon flesh. Blend until smooth, adding the remaining syrup and lime juice to taste.

3 Pour the mixture into a bowl and stir in the shredded basil. Chill until required. Serve garnished with whole basil leaves and the reserved melon balls.

Red Onion and Beet Soup

This beautiful, ruby-red soup, with its contrasting swirl of yogurt, looks stunning at any dinner party.

INGREDIENTS

Serves 4 to 6

1 tablespoon olive oil

2½ cups sliced red onions

2 garlic cloves, crushed

2½ cups cooked beets, cut into sticks

1¼ quarts vegetable stock or water

1 cup cooked soup pasta

2 tablespoons raspberry vinegar

salt and freshly ground black pepper

plain yogurt or fromage blanc and
snipped fresh chives, to garnish

2 Cook slowly for about 20 minutes, or until soft and tender, stirring occasionally.

3 Add the beets, stock or water, cooked pasta, and vinegar and heat through. Season and garnish with swirls of yogurt or fromage blanc and chives.

1 Heat the olive oil in a large saucepan or flameproof casserole. Add the onions and garlic.

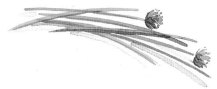

COOK'S TIP

Substituting cooked barley for the pasta gives extra nuttiness to the flavor.

Beet Soup with Ravioli

Beets and pasta make an unusual combination, but this soup is no less good for that.

Serves 4 to 6

1 quantity of basic pasta dough (see page 232 for recipe and directions)

1 egg white, beaten, for brushing

all-purpose flour for dusting

1 small onion or shallot, minced

2 garlic cloves, crushed

1 teaspoon fennel seeds

2½ cups chicken or vegetable stock

8 ounces cooked beets

2 tablespoons fresh orange juice

fresh fennel or dill leaves, to garnish

crusty bread, to serve

For the filling

1½ cups finely chopped mushrooms

1 shallot or small onion, minced

1 or 2 garlic cloves, crushed

1 teaspoon chopped fresh thyme

1 tablespoon chopped fresh parsley

6 tablespoons fresh white bread crumbs

salt and freshly ground black pepper

a large pinch of freshly grated nutmeg

1 Put all the filling ingredients in a food processor or blender and process to a paste.

2 Roll the pasta into thin sheets. Lay one piece over a ravioli tray and put 1 teaspoon of the filling into each depression. Brush around the edges of each ravioli with egg white. Cover with another sheet of pasta and press the edges together well to seal. Transfer to a floured dish towel and rest for one hour before cooking.

3 Cut into individual ravioli. Cook in a large pan of boiling, salted water for 2 minutes: Cook in batches to stop them sticking together. Remove and drop into a bowl of cold water for 5 seconds before placing on a tray. (You can make the ravioli a day in advance and keep in the refrigerator.)

4 Put the onion, garlic, and fennel seeds into a pan with ⅔ cup of the stock and bring to a boil. Lower the heat, cover, and simmer for 5 minutes until tender. Peel and finely dice the beet, reserving 4 tablespoons for the garnish. Add the rest of it to the soup with the remaining stock and bring to a boil.

5 Add the orange juice and cooked ravioli and simmer for 2 minutes. Serve in shallow soup bowls, garnished with the reserved diced beet and fresh fennel or dill leaves. Serve hot, with crusty bread.

Italian Vegetable Soup

The success of this clear soup depends on the quality of the stock, so use homemade vegetable stock rather than bouillon cubes.

INGREDIENTS

Serves 4

1 small carrot

l baby leek

1 celery stalk

2 ounces green cabbage

3¾ cups vegetable stock

1 bay leaf

1 cup cooked cannellini beans

¼ cup soup pasta, such as tiny shells, bows, stars, or elbows

salt and freshly ground black pepper

snipped fresh chives, to garnish

1 Cut the carrot, leek, and celery into 2-inch long julienne strips. Finely shred the cabbage.

2 Put the stock and bay leaf into a large saucepan and bring to a boil. Add the carrot, leek, and celery, cover, and simmer for 6 minutes, until the vegetables are soft, but not tender.

3 Add the cabbage, beans, and pasta and simmer, uncovered, for 4–5 minutes longer, or until the vegetables are tender and the pasta is *al dente*.

4 Remove the bay leaf and season to taste. Ladle the soup into four warm soup bowls and garnish with snipped chives. Serve immediately.

Butternut Squash Bisque

This is a fragrant, creamy and delicately flavored soup.

INGREDIENTS

Serves 4

2 tablespoons butter or margarine

2 small onions, minced

3 cups peeled, seeded, and cubed
   butternut squash

1¼ quarts chicken stock

1½ cups cubed potatoes

1 teaspoon paprika

½ cup whipping cream (optional)

1½ tablespoons snipped fresh chives, plus
   a few whole chives, to garnish

salt and freshly ground black pepper

1 Melt the butter or margarine in a large saucepan. Add the onions and cook for about 5 minutes until soft.

2 Add the squash, stock, potatoes, and paprika and bring to a boil. Lower the heat to low, cover the pan, and simmer for about 35 minutes until all the vegetables are soft.

3 Pour the soup into a food processor or blender and process until smooth. Return the soup to the pan and stir in the cream, if using. Season with salt and pepper and reheat slowly.

4 Stir in the chopped chives just before serving. Garnish each serving with a few whole chives.

Red Pepper Soup with Lime

The beautiful, rich red color of this soup makes it an attractive appetizer or light lunch. For a special dinner, toast some tiny croutons and serve these sprinkled into the soup.

INGREDIENTS

Serves 4 to 6

1 large onion, chopped

4 red bell peppers, seeded and chopped

1 teaspoon olive oil

1 garlic clove, crushed

1 small fresh red chili, sliced

3 tablespoons tomato paste

3¾ cups chicken stock

finely grated peel and juice of 1 lime

salt and freshly ground black pepper

shreds of lime peel, to garnish

1 Cook the onion and peppers slowly in the oil in a covered saucepan for about 5 minutes, shaking the pan occasionally, until just soft.

2 Stir in the garlic, chili, and tomato paste. Add half the stock and bring to a boil. Cover and simmer for 10 minutes.

3 Leave to cool slightly. Purée in a food processor or blender. Return to the pan and add the remaining stock, the lime peel and juice, and salt and pepper.

4 Return the soup to a boil. Serve at once, with a few strips of lime peel scattered into each bowl.

Tomato and Fresh Basil Soup

This is the perfect soup for late summer when fresh tomatoes are at their most flavorsome.

INGREDIENTS

Serves 4 to 6

1 tablespoon olive oil

2 tablespoons butter

1 onion, minced

2 pounds ripe Italian plum tomatoes, roughly chopped

1 garlic clove, roughly chopped

about 3 cups chicken or vegetable stock

1/2 cup dry white wine

2 tablespoons sun-dried tomato paste

2 tablespoons shredded fresh basil, plus a few whole leaves, to garnish

2/3 cup heavy cream

salt and freshly ground black pepper

1 Heat the oil and butter in a large saucepan until foaming. Add the onion and cook slowly for about 5 minutes, stirring frequently, until soft, but do not let brown.

2 Stir in the tomatoes and garlic, stock, white wine, and sun-dried tomato paste, with salt and pepper to taste. Bring to a boil. Lower the heat, half-cover the pan, and simmer slowly for 20 minutes, stirring occasionally to stop the tomatoes from sticking to the bottom.

3 Process the soup with the shredded basil in a food processor or blender. Press through a strainer into the rinsed pan.

4 Add the heavy cream and heat through, stirring: Do not let the soup approach the boiling point. Check the consistency and add more stock, if necessary. Adjust the seasoning to taste, pour into warm bowls, and garnish with whole basil leaves. Serve at once.

Wild Mushroom Soup

Wild mushrooms are expensive. Dried porcini have an intense flavor, so only a small quantity is needed. The beef stock may seem unusual in a vegetable soup, but it helps to strengthen the earthy flavor of the mushrooms.

INGREDIENTS

Serves 4

2 cups dried porcini mushrooms

1 cup warm water

2 tablespoons olive oil

1 tablespoon butter

2 leeks, finely sliced

2 shallots, roughly chopped

1 garlic clove, roughly chopped

8 ounces fresh wild mushrooms

1¼ quarts beef stock

½ teaspoon dried thyme

⅔ cup heavy cream

salt and freshly ground black pepper

sprigs of fresh thyme, to garnish

3 Chop or slice the fresh mushrooms and add to the pan. Stir over medium heat for a few minutes until they begin to soften. Pour in the beef stock and bring to a boil. Add the porcini, soaking liquid, dried thyme, and salt and pepper. Lower the heat, half-cover the pan, and simmer slowly for 30 minutes, stirring occasionally.

4 Pour about three-quarters of the soup into a food processor or blender and process until smooth. Return to the soup remaining in the pan, stir in the heavy cream, and heat through. Check the consistency, adding more stock or water if the soup is too thick. Adjust the seasoning. Serve hot, garnished with sprigs of fresh thyme.

1 Put the dried porcini in a bowl, add the warm water, and leave to soak for 20 to 30 minutes. Lift out of the liquid and squeeze to remove as much of the soaking liquid as possible. Strain all the liquid and reserve to use later. Finely chop the porcini.

2 Heat the oil and butter in a large saucepan until foaming. Add the leeks, shallots, and garlic and cook slowly for about 5 minutes, stirring frequently, until soft but not colored.

Hungarian Sour Cherry Soup

V

Particularly popular in summer, this fruit soup is typical of Hungarian cuisine. The recipe makes good use of the plump, sour cherries available locally. Fruit soups are thickened with flour, and a touch of salt is added to help bring out the flavor of the cold soup.

INGREDIENTS

Serves 4

1 tablespoon all-purpose flour

½ cup sour cream

a generous pinch of salt

1 teaspoon sugar

1½ cups fresh sour or morello cherries, pitted

3¾ cups water

¼ cup sugar

1 In a bowl, blend the flour with the sour cream until smooth. Add the salt and sugar.

2 Put the cherries in a pan with the water and sugar. Slowly poach for about 10 minutes.

3 Remove from the heat and set aside 2 tablespoons of the cooking liquid as a garnish. Stir another 2 tablespoons of the cherry liquid into the flour and sour cream mixture. Pour this onto the cherries.

4 Return to the heat and bring to a boil. Lower the heat and simmer for 5 to 6 minutes.

5 Remove from the heat, cover with plastic wrap, and leave to cool. Add extra salt if necessary. Serve with the reserved cooking liquid swirled in.

Apple Soup

Romania has vast fruit orchards, and this traditional soup is a delicious result of that natural resource.

INGREDIENTS

Serves 6

3 tablespoons oil

1 kohlrabi, diced

3 carrots, diced

2 celery stalks, diced

1 green bell pepper, seeded and diced

2 tomatoes, diced

2¼ quarts chicken stock

6 large green apples

3 tablespoons all-purpose flour

⅔ cup heavy cream

1 tablespoon sugar

2 to 3 tablespoons lemon juice

salt and freshly ground black pepper

lemon wedges and crusty bread, to serve

1 Heat the oil in a large saucepan. Add the kohlrabi, carrots, celery, green pepper, and tomatoes and fry for 5 to 6 minutes until just soft.

2 Pour in the chicken stock and bring to a boil. Lower the heat and simmer for about 45 minutes.

3 Meanwhile, peel and core the apples, then chop into small dice. Add to the pan and simmer for 15 minutes longer.

4 In a bowl, mix together the flour and cream. Slowly pour into the soup, stirring well, and bring to a boil. Add the sugar and lemon juice before seasoning. Serve at once with lemon wedges and crusty bread.

[V]

Hot-and-Sour Soup

A classic Chinese soup, this is a warming and flavorsome start to any meal.

INGREDIENTS

Serves 4

¼ ounce dried cloud ears

8 fresh shiitake mushrooms

3 ounces firm tofu

½ cup sliced and drained canned
   bamboo shoots

3¾ cups vegetable stock

1 tablespoon sugar

3 tablespoons rice vinegar

1 tablespoon light soy sauce

¼ teaspoon chili oil

½ teaspoon salt

a large pinch of freshly ground white
   pepper

1 tablespoon cornstarch

1 tablespoon cold water

1 egg white

1 teaspoon sesame oil

2 scallions, cut into fine rings,
   to garnish

COOK'S TIP

To transform this tasty soup into
a nutritious light meal, simply
add extra mushrooms, tofu
and bamboo shoots.

1 Soak the cloud ears in hot water for 30 minutes, or until soft. Drain, trim off, and discard the hard base from each, and chop the cloud ears roughly.

2 Remove and discard the stems from the shiitake mushrooms. Cut the caps into thin strips. Cut the tofu into ½-inch cubes, and shred the bamboo shoots finely.

3 Place the stock, mushrooms, tofu, bamboo shoots, and cloud ears in a large saucepan. Bring the stock to a boil, lower the heat, and simmer for about 5 minutes.

4 Stir in the sugar, vinegar, soy sauce, chili oil, and salt and pepper. Stir the cornstarch to a paste with the water. Add the mixture to the soup, stirring until the soup thickens slightly.

5 Lightly beat the egg white, then pour it slowly into the soup in a steady stream, stirring constantly. Cook, stirring, until the egg white changes color.

6 Add the sesame oil just before serving. Ladle into warm bowls and garnish each portion with scallion rings.

Pear and Watercress Soup

This unusual soup combines sweet pears with slightly sharp watercress. A more traditional partner, Stilton cheese, appears in the form of crisp croutons.

INGREDIENTS

Serves 6

1 bunch of watercress

4 pears, sliced

3¾ cups chicken stock, preferably
   homemade

½ cup heavy cream

juice of 1 lime

salt and freshly ground black pepper

For the Stilton croutons

2 tablespoons butter

1 tablespoon olive oil

3 cups cubed day-old bread

1 cup crumbled Stilton cheese

1 Place two-thirds of the watercress leaves and all the stems in a pan with the pears, stock, and a little seasoning. Simmer for 15 to 20 minutes.

2 Reserving some of the watercress leaves for the garnish, add the rest to the soup and immediately blend in a food processor until smooth.

3 Put the soup into a bowl and stir in the cream and the lime juice to mix the flavors thoroughly. Season again to taste. Pour all the soup back into the rinsed pan and reheat, stirring gently, until warmed through.

4 To make the Stilton croutons, melt the butter and oil. Add the bread cubes and fry until golden brown. Drain on paper towels. Put the cheese on top and heat under a hot broiler until bubbling.

5 Pour the soup into warm bowls. Divide the croutons and reserved watercress between the bowls and serve.

Stargazer Vegetable Soup

V

If you have the time, it is worth making your own stock— either vegetable or, if preferred, chicken or fish—for this recipe.

INGREDIENTS

Serves 4

1 yellow bell pepper

2 large zucchini

2 large carrots

1 kohlrabi

3¾ cups well-flavored vegetable stock

2 ounces rice vermicelli

salt and freshly ground black pepper

1 Cut the pepper into quarters and remove the seeds and core. Cut the zucchini and carrots lengthways into ¼-inch slices. Slice the kohlrabi into ¼-inch slices.

2 Using tiny aspic or cookie cutters, stamp out shapes from the vegetables. Or, use a very sharp knife to cut the sliced vegetables into stars and other decorative shapes.

COOK'S TIP

Sauté the leftover vegetable pieces in a little oil and mix with cooked brown rice to make a rice dish.

3 Place the vegetables and stock in a pan and bring to the boil. Lower the heat and simmer for 10 minutes until the vegetables are tender. Season to taste with salt and pepper.

4 Meanwhile, place the vermicelli in a bowl and cover with boiling water; set aside for 4 minutes. Drain well. Divide between 4 warm soup bowls and ladle the soup over. Serve.

V

Spinach and Rice Soup

Use very fresh, young spinach leaves and risotto rice to prepare this surprisingly light, refreshing soup.

INGREDIENTS

Serves 4

1½ pounds fresh spinach, washed

3 tablespoons extra-virgin olive oil

1 small onion, minced

2 garlic cloves, minced

1 small fresh red chili, seeded and minced

generous ½ cup risotto rice

1¼ quarts vegetable stock

salt and freshly ground black pepper

4 tablespoons grated Pecorino cheese,
    to serve

1 Place the spinach in a large pan with just the water that clings to its leaves after washing. Add a large pinch of salt and heat gently until the spinach wilts. Remove from the heat and drain, reserving any liquid.

2 Either chop the spinach finely using a knife or place in a food processor and purée coarsely.

3 Heat the oil in a large saucepan. Add the onion, garlic, and chili and cook for 4 to 5 minutes until soft. Stir in the rice until well coated. Pour in the stock and reserved spinach liquid.

4 Bring to a boil. Lower the heat and simmer for 10 minutes. Add the spinach and cook for 5 to 7 minutes longer, until the rice is tender. Season with salt and freshly ground pepper. Serve with the Pecorino cheese.

Broccoli, Anchovy, and Pasta Soup

This soup is from Apulia in the south of Italy, where anchovies and broccoli are often used together.

INGREDIENTS

Serves 4

2 tablespoons olive oil

1 small onion, minced

1 garlic clove, minced

¼ to ⅓ fresh red chili, seeded and minced

2 canned anchovy fillets, drained

scant 1 cup passata (strained, puréed tomatoes)

3 tablespoons dry white wine

1¼ quarts vegetable stock

2 cups broccoli flowerets

1¾ cups *orecchiette*

salt and freshly ground black pepper

grated Pecorino cheese, to serve

1 Heat the oil in a large saucepan. Add the onion, garlic, chili, and anchovies and cook over low heat, stirring all the time, for 5 to 6 minutes.

2 Add the passata and wine, with salt and pepper to taste, and bring to a boil. Cover the pan and cook over low heat, stirring occasionally, for 12 to 15 minutes.

3 Pour in the stock and return to a boil. Add the broccoli and simmer for about 5 minutes. Add the pasta and return to a boil, stirring. Lower the heat and simmer for 7 to 8 minutes, or according to the directions on the package, stirring frequently, until the pasta is *al dente*.

4 Taste and adjust the seasoning. Serve hot, in warm bowls. Hand around the grated Pecorino cheese separately.

Consommé with Agnolotti

Shrimp, crab, and chicken jostle for the upper hand in this rich and satisfying consommé.

INGREDIENTS

Serves 4 to 6

3 ounces cooked shelled shrimp

3 ounces canned crabmeat, drained

1 teaspoon finely grated fresh ginger root

1 tablespoon fresh white bread crumbs

1 teaspoon light soy sauce

1 scallion, minced

1 garlic clove, crushed

1 egg white, beaten

14-ounce can chicken or fish consommé

2 tablespoons sherry or vermouth

salt and freshly ground black pepper

For the pasta

1¾ cups all-purpose flour

pinch of salt

2 eggs

2 teaspoons cold water

For the garnish

2 ounces cooked shelled shrimp

fresh cilantro leaves

1 To make the pasta, sift the flour and salt onto a clean work surface and make a well in the center with your hand.

2 Put the eggs and water into the well. Using a fork, beat the eggs gently together, gradually drawing in the flour from the sides to make a thick paste.

3 When the mixture becomes too stiff to use a fork, use your hands to mix to a firm dough. Knead the dough for about 5 minutes until smooth. Wrap in plastic wrap to prevent it from drying out and leave to rest for 20 to 30 minutes.

4 Meanwhile, put the shrimp, crabmeat, ginger, bread crumbs, soy sauce, scallion, garlic, and seasoning into a food processor or blender and process until smooth.

5 Once the pasta has rested, roll it into thin sheets. Stamp out 32 circles 2 inches in diameter, using a fluted cookie cutter.

6 Place 1 teaspoon of the filling in the center of half the pasta circles. Brush the edge of each circle with egg white and sandwich with a second circle on top. Pinch the edges together to stop the filling seeping out.

7 Cook the pasta in a large pan of boiling, salted water for 5 minutes: Cook in batches to stop them sticking together. Remove and drop into a bowl of cold water for 5 seconds before placing on a tray. (You can make these pasta shapes a day in advance. Cover with plastic wrap and store in the refrigerator.)

8 Heat the consommé in a pan with the sherry or vermouth. Add the cooked pasta shapes and simmer for 1 to 2 minutes.

9 Serve the pasta in soup bowls covered with hot consommé. Garnish with shelled shrimp and cilantro leaves.

Oyster Soup

Oysters make this delicious soup really special.

INGREDIENTS

Serves 6

2 cups milk

2 cups light cream

5 cups shucked oysters, drained, with their
   juice reserved

a pinch of paprika

2 tablespoons butter

salt and freshly ground black pepper

1 tablespoon chopped fresh parsley,
   to garnish

1 Combine the milk, light cream, and oyster juice in a heavy-bottomed saucepan.

2 Heat the mixture over medium heat until small bubbles appear around the edge of the pan, being careful not to let it boil. Lower the heat to low and add the oysters.

3 Cook, stirring occasionally, until the oysters plump up and their edges begin to curl. Add the paprika and season to taste.

4 Meanwhile, warm 6 soup bowls. Cut the butter into 6 pieces and put one piece in each bowl.

5 Ladle the oyster soup in and sprinkle with chopped parsley. Serve at once.

Asparagus Soup with Crab

A beautiful, green soup with the pure taste of fresh asparagus. The crab is added at the last moment as a luxurious garnish.

INGREDIENTS

Serves 6 to 8

3 to 3½ pounds fresh asparagus

2 tablespoons butter

1½ quarts chicken stock

2 tablespoons cornstarch

2 to 3 tablespoons cold water

½ cup whipping cream

salt and freshly ground black pepper

6 to 7 ounces white crabmeat,
    to garnish

1 Trim the woody ends from the bottom of the asparagus spears and cut the spears into l-inch pieces.

2 Melt the butter in a heavy saucepan or flameproof casserole over medium-high heat. Add the asparagus and cook for 5 to 6 minutes, stirring frequently, until it is bright green.

3 Add the stock and bring to a boil over high heat, skimming off any foam from the surface. Lower the heat and simmer over medium heat for 3 to 5 minutes until the asparagus is tender, yet crisp. Reserve 12 to 16 of the asparagus tips for the garnish. Season the soup, cover, and continue simmering for 15 to 20 minutes until the asparagus is very tender.

4 Purée the soup in a blender or food processor and pass the mixture through the fine blade of a food mill back into the saucepan. Return the soup to a boil over medium-high heat. Blend the cornstarch with the water and whisk into the boiling soup to thicken. Stir in the cream and adjust the seasoning.

5 To serve, ladle the soup into bowls and top each with a spoonful of the crabmeat and a few of the reserved asparagus tips.

Clam Chowder

Canned or bottled clams in brine, once drained, can be used as an alternative to fresh ones in their shells. Discard any clam shells that remain closed during cooking because this means they were already dead.

INGREDIENTS

Serves 4

1¼ cups heavy cream

6 tablespoons unsalted butter

1 small onion, minced

1 apple, cored and sliced

1 garlic clove, crushed

3 tablespoons mild curry powder

3 cups baby corn cobs

8 ounces cooked new potatoes

24 boiled pearl onions

2½ cups fish stock

40 small clams

salt and freshly ground black pepper

8 lime wedges, to garnish (optional)

3 In another saucepan, melt the remaining butter and add the baby corn, potatoes, and pearl onions. Cook for 5 minutes. Increase the heat and add the cream mixture and stock. Bring to a boil.

4 Add the clams. Cover and cook until the clams open: Discard any that do not open. Season to taste with salt and freshly ground black pepper. Serve, garnished with lime wedges, if liked.

1 Pour the cream into a small saucepan and cook over high heat until it reduces by half.

2 In a larger pan, melt half the butter. Add the onion, apple, garlic, and curry powder and sauté until the onion is translucent. Add the reduced cream and stir well.

Saffron-Mussel Soup

This is one of France's most delicious seafood soups. For everyday eating, the French serve all the mussels in their shells. Serve with plenty of French bread.

INGREDIENTS

Serves 4 to 6

3 tablespoons unsalted butter

8 shallots, minced

1 bouquet garni

1 teaspoon black peppercorns

1½ cups dry white wine

2¼ pounds mussels, scrubbed and debearded

2 leeks, trimmed and minced

1 fennel bulb, minced

1 carrot, minced

several saffron strands

1 quart fish or chicken stock

2 to 3 tablespoons cornstarch, blended with 3 tablespoons cold water

½ cup whipping cream

1 tomato, peeled, seeded, and finely diced

2 tablespoons Pernod or other anise-flavored liquor (optional)

salt and freshly ground black pepper

1 In a large, heavy-bottomed pan, melt half the butter over medium-high heat. Add half the shallots and cook for 1 to 2 minutes until softe but not colored. Add the bouquet garni, peppercorns, and white wine and bring to a boil. Add the mussels, cover tightly and cook over high heat for 3 to 5 minutes, shaking the pan from time to time, until the mussels open.

2 Using a slotted spoon, transfer the mussels to a bowl. Strain the cooking liquid through a cheesecloth-lined strainer; reserve.

3 Pull open the shells and remove most of the mussels. Discard any closed mussels.

4 Melt the remaining butter over medium heat. Add the remaining shallots and cook for 1 to 2 minutes. Add the leeks, fennel, carrot, and saffron and cook for 3 to 5 minutes.

5 Stir in the reserved cooking liquid, bring to a boil, and cook for 5 minutes until the vegetables are tender and the liquid reduces slightly. Add the stock and bring to a boil, skimming any foam from the surface. Season with salt, if needed, and black pepper and cook for 5 minutes longer.

6 Stir the blended cornstarch into the soup. Simmer for 2 to 3 minutes until the soup is slightly thickened. Stir in the cream, mussels and, chopped tomato. Stir in the Pernod, if using, and cook for 1 to 2 minutes until hot. Serve at once.

Seafood-Won-Ton Soup

This is a variation on the popular won-ton soup that is traditionally prepared using pork.

INGREDIENTS

Serves 4

2 ounces raw jumbo shrimp or
    tiger prawns

2 ounces queen scallops

3 ounces skinless cod fillet, roughly chopped

1 tablespoon finely snipped fresh chives

1 teaspoon dry sherry

1 small egg white, lightly beaten

½ teaspoon sesame oil

¼ teaspoon salt

large pinch of ground white pepper

20 won-ton wrappers

2 Romaine lettuce leaves, shredded

3¾ cups fish stock

fresh cilantro leaves and garlic chives,
    to garnish

1 Peel and devein the shrimp. Rinse, dry on paper towels, and cut into small pieces.

2 Rinse and dry the scallops. Chop them into small pieces the same size as the shrimp.

3 Place the cod in a food processor and process until a paste forms. Scrape into a bowl and stir in the shrimp, scallops, chives, sherry, egg white, sesame oil, and salt and pepper. Mix well, cover, and leave in a cool place to marinate for 20 minutes.

4 Make the won-tons. Place 1 teaspoon of the seafood filling in the center of a won-ton wrapper. Bring the corners together to meet at the top and twist together to enclose the filling. Fill the remaining won-ton wrappers in the same way. Tie with a fresh chive if desired.

COOK'S TIP

The filled won-ton skins can be made ahead and frozen for several weeks. Cook them straight from the freezer.

5 Bring a large saucepan of water to a boil. Drop in the won-tons. When the water returns to a boil, lower the heat and simmer for 5 minutes, or until the won-tons float to the surface. Drain the won-tons and divide them between 4 warm soup bowls.

6 Add a portion of lettuce to each bowl. Bring the fish stock to a boil. Ladle it on top of the lettuce and garnish each portion with cilantro leaves and garlic chives. Serve at once.

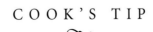

Lobster Bisque

The blue and black clawed lobster is known as the king of the shellfish. When cooked, its shell turns a brilliant red. This is an extravagant soup, worthy of a celebration dinner party.

INGREDIENTS

Serves 4

1 cooked lobster, about 1½ pounds
2 tablespoons vegetable oil
½ cup butter
2 shallots, minced
juice of ½ lemon
3 tablespoons brandy
1 bay leaf
1 sprig of fresh parsley, plus extra
    to garnish
1 blade of mace
1¼ quarts fish stock
3 tablespoons all-purpose flour
3 tablespoons heavy cream
salt and freshly ground black pepper
a pinch of cayenne pepper, to garnish

1 Preheat the oven to 350°F. Lay the lobster out flat and split in half lengthwise. Remove and discard the little stomach sac from the head, the threadlike intestine, and the coral, if any.

2 In a large, heavy-bottomed roasting pan, heat the oil with 2 tablespoons of the butter. Sauté the lobster, flesh-side down, for 5 minutes. Add the shallots, lemon juice, and brandy and roast for 15 minutes.

3 Remove the lobster meat from the shell. Place the shell and the juices in a large saucepan and simmer with the bay leaf, parsley, mace, and stock for 30 minutes; strain. Finely chop 1 tablespoon of the lobster meat. Process the rest with 3 tablespoons of the butter.

4 Melt the remaining butter. Add the flour and cook slowly for 30 seconds. Add the stock gradually and bring to a boil, stirring constantly. Stir in the processed meat, the cream, and seasoning to taste.

5 Ladle into warm soup bowls and garnish with chopped lobster, parsley sprigs, and a sprinkling of cayenne. Serve at once, piping hot.

Shrimp and Egg-Knot Soup

An unusual and special soup, just right for a festive occasion.

INGREDIENTS

Serves 4

3¾ cups kombu and bonito stock or
   instant dashi, prepared
1 teaspoon soy sauce
a dash of sake or dry white wine
salt
1 scallion, finely sliced, to garnish

For the shrimp shinjo balls
7 ounces jumbo shrimp, shelled, thawed
   if frozen
2½ ounces cod fillet, skinned
1 teaspoon egg white
1 teaspoon sake or dry white wine
4½ teaspoons cornstarch or potato
   flour
2 or 3 drops of soy sauce

For the omelet
1 egg, beaten
a dash of mirin
vegetable oil for frying

1 Devein the shrimp. Process the shrimp, cod, egg white, sake or wine, cornstarch or potato flour, soy sauce and a pinch of salt in a food processor or blender to make a sticky paste. Alternatively, finely chop the shrimp and cod, crush them with the knife's blade and then pound them well in a mortar and pestle, before adding the remaining ingredients.

2 Shape the mixture into 4 balls and steam them for 10 minutes over high heat. Meanwhile, soak the scallion for the garnish in cold water for 5 minutes; drain.

3 To make the omelet, mix the egg with a pinch of salt and the mirin. Heat a little oil in a skillet. Pour in the egg, tilting the pan to coat it evenly. When the egg has set, turn the omelet over and cook for 30 seconds longer. Leave to cool.

4 Cut the omelet into long strips about ¾-inch wide. Knot each strip once, place in a strainer, and rinse with hot water to remove the excess oil. Bring the stock to a boil. Add the soy sauce, a pinch of salt, and a dash of sake or wine. Divide the shrimp balls and the egg knots between 4 warm bowls. Pour in the soup and sprinkle with the scallion. Serve at once.

Thai Fish Soup

Thai fish sauce, or nam pla, *is rich in B vitamins and is used extensively in Thai cooking. It is sold at Thai or Indonesian stores and good supermarkets.*

INGREDIENTS

Serves 4

12 ounces raw jumbo shrimp

1 tablespoon peanut oil

1¼ quarts well-flavored chicken or
    fish stock

1 lemongrass stalk, bruised and cut into
    1-inch pieces

2 kaffir lime leaves, torn into pieces

juice and finely grated peel of 1 lime

½ fresh green chili, seeded and finely
    sliced

4 scallops

24 mussels, scrubbed

4 ounces monkfish fillet, cut into
    ¾-inch chunks

2 teaspoons fish sauce

For the garnish

1 kaffir lime leaf, shredded

½ fresh red chili, finely sliced

1 Peel the shrimp, reserving the shells. Remove the black vein running along their backs.

2 Heat the oil in a saucepan. Add the shrimp shells and fry until they turn pink. Add the stock, lemongrass, lime leaves, lime peel, and green chili. Bring to a boil. Simmer for 20 minutes, then strain through a strainer, reserving the liquid.

3 Prepare the scallops by cutting them in half, leaving the corals attached to one half.

4 Discard any open mussels that do not close when tapped. Return the stock to the rinsed pan. Add the shrimp, mussels, monkfish, and scallops and cook for 3 minutes. Remove from the heat and discard any closed mussels. Add the lime juice and fish sauce. Serve garnished with the shredded lime leaf and finely sliced red chili.

Seafarer's Stew

Any variety of firm fish may be used in this recipe, but be sure to use smoked haddock as well; it is essential for its distinctive flavor.

INGREDIENTS

Serves 4

20 mussels, scrubbed

8 ounces undyed smoked haddock fillet

8 ounces fresh monkfish fillet

2 bacon slices (optional)

1 tablespoon olive oil

1 shallot, minced

2 cups coarsely grated carrots

⅔ cup light or heavy cream

4 ounces cooked shelled shrimp

salt and freshly ground black pepper

2 tablespoons chopped fresh parsley, to garnish

1 Discard any open mussels that do not close when tapped. In a large, heavy-based pan, simmer the haddock and monkfish in 1¼ quarts water for 5 minutes. Add the mussels and cover the pan with a lid.

2 Cook for 5 minutes longer, or until all the mussels are open. Discard any that have not opened. Drain, reserving the liquid. Return the liquid to the rinsed pan and set aside.

3 Flake the haddock coarsely, removing any skin and bones, then cut the monkfish into large chunks. Cut the bacon, if using, into strips.

4 Heat the oil in a heavy-based frying pan and fry the shallot and bacon for 3 to 4 minutes or until the shallot is soft and the bacon lightly browned. Add to the strained fish broth, bring to a boil, then add the grated carrots and cook for 10 minutes.

5 Stir in the cream together with the haddock, monkfish, mussels and shrimp and heat gently, without boiling. Season and serve in large bowls, garnished with parsley.

Corn and Crab Bisque

This is a Louisiana classic, which is certainly luxurious enough for a dinner party so it is worth the extra time required to prepare the fresh crab. The crab shells together with the corn cobs, from which the kernels are stripped, make a fine-flavored stock.

INGREDIENTS

Serves 8

4 large corn cobs

2 bay leaves

1 cooked crab, about 2¼ pounds

2 tablespoons butter

2 tablespoons all-purpose flour

1¼ cups whipping cream

6 scallions, shredded

a pinch of cayenne pepper

salt and freshly ground black and white pepper

hot French bread or breadsticks, to serve

1 Pull away the husks and silk from the cobs of corn and strip off the kernels.

2 Keep the kernels on one side and put the stripped cobs into a deep saucepan or flameproof casserole with 3 quarts cold water, the bay leaves, and 2 teaspoons salt. Bring to a boil and leave to simmer while you prepare the crab.

3 Pull away the 2 flaps between the big claws of the crab, stand it on its "nose", where the flaps were, and bang down firmly with the heel of your hand on the rounded end.

4 Separate the crab from its top shell, keeping the shell.

5 Push out the crab's mouth and its abdominal sac immediately below the mouth; discard both.

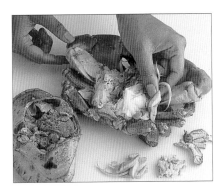

6 Pull away the feathery gills surrounding the central chamber; discard. Scrape out all the semiliquid brown meat from the shell; set aside.

7 Crack the claws in as many places as necessary to extract all the white meat. Pick out the white meat from the fragile cavities in the central body of the crab. Set aside all the crabmeat, brown and white. Put the spidery legs, back shell, and all the other pieces of shell into the pan with the corn cobs. Simmer for 15 minutes longer. Strain the stock into a clean pan and boil hard to reduce to 2¼ quarts.

8 Meanwhile, melt the butter in a small pan. Sprinkle in the flour and stir constantly over low heat until the roux is the color of rich cream.

9 Off the heat, slowly stir in 1 cup of the stock. Return the pan to the heat and stir until the roux thickens. Stir the thick roux into the pan of strained stock.

10 Add the corn kernels, return to a boil, and simmer for 5 minutes.

11 Add the crabmeat, cream, and scallions and season with cayenne and salt and pepper (preferably a mixture of black and white). Return to a boil and simmer for 2 minutes longer. Serve with hot French bread or breadsticks.

Seafood Soup with Rouille

This is a really chunky, aromatic mixed fish soup from France, flavored with plenty of saffron and herbs. Rouille, the fiery hot paste, is served separately for everyone to swirl into their soup to taste.

INGREDIENTS

Serves 6

3 red mullet, scaled and dressed

12 large shrimp

1½ pounds white fish, such as cod, haddock, halibut, or monkfish

8 ounces mussels

1 onion, quartered

1¼ quarts water

1 teaspoon saffron strands

5 tablespoons olive oil

1 fennel bulb, roughly chopped

4 garlic cloves, crushed

3 strips pared orange peel

4 sprigs of thyme

1½ pounds tomatoes, or 14-ounce can crushed tomatoes

2 tablespoons sun-dried tomato paste

3 bay leaves

salt and freshly ground black pepper

For the rouille

1 red bell pepper, seeded and roughly chopped

1 fresh red chili, seeded and sliced

2 garlic cloves, chopped

5 tablespoons olive oil

¼ cup fresh bread crumbs

1 To make the *rouille*, process the pepper, chili, garlic, oil and bread crumbs in a blender or food processor until smooth. Transfer to a serving dish and chill.

COOK'S TIP

To save time, order the fish in advance and ask the fishmonger to fillet the mullet for you.

2 Fillet the mullet by cutting away the flesh from the backbone, reserving the heads and bones. Cut the fillets into small chunks. Shell half the shrimp and reserve the trimmings to make the stock. Skin the white fish, discarding any bones, and cut into large chunks. Scrub the mussels well, discarding any open ones.

3 Put the fish and shrimp trimmings in a saucepan with the onion and water and bring to a boil. Lower the heat and simmer for 30 minutes. Cool slightly and strain.

4 Soak the saffron in 1 tablespoon boiling water. Heat 2 tablespoons of the oil in a large sauté pan or saucepan. Add the mullet and white fish and fry over a high heat for 1 minute. Drain.

5 Heat the remaining oil in the pan. Add the fennel, garlic, orange peel, and thyme and fry until they begin to color. Make up the strained stock to about 1¼ quarts with water.

6 If using fresh tomatoes, plunge them into boiling water for 30 seconds, then refresh in cold water. Peel and chop. Add the stock to the pan with the saffron, tomatoes, tomato paste and bay leaves. Season and bring almost to a boil. Simmer, covered, for 20 minutes.

7 Stir in the mullet, white fish, shelled and unshelled shrimp, and the mussels. Cover the pan and cook for 3 to 4 minutes. Discard any mussels that do not open. Serve the soup hot with the *rouille*.

Creamy Cod Chowder

The sharp flavor of the smoked cod adds depth to this creamy soup. Serve this soup as a substantial first course before a light main course. Warm, crusty whole wheat bread goes well with it.

INGREDIENTS

Serves 4 to 6

12 ounces smoked cod fillet

1 small onion, minced

1 bay leaf

4 black peppercorns

3¾ cups milk

2 teaspoons cornstarch

2 teaspoons cold water

7-ounce can whole corn kernels

1 tablespoon chopped fresh parsley

crusty whole wheat bread, to serve

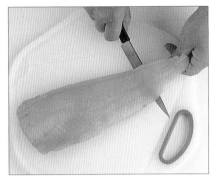

1 Skin the fish with a knife and put into a large saucepan with the onion, bay leaf, black peppercorns, and milk.

2 Bring to a boil. Lower the heat and simmer very slowly for 12 to 15 minutes, or until the fish is just cooked: Do not overcook.

3 Using a slotted spoon, lift out the fish and flake into large chunks. Remove and discard the bay leaf and peppercorns.

4 Blend the cornstarch with the water carefully until it forms a smooth paste. Add to the saucepan and bring to a boil. Lower the heat and simmer for 1 minute, or until slightly thick.

5 Drain the corn kernels and add to the saucepan together with the flaked fish and chopped fresh parsley.

6 Reheat the soup until piping hot, taking care that the fish does not disintegrate: Do not boil. Ladle into 4 or 6 soup bowls and serve at once with plenty of warm whole wheat bread.

COOK'S TIP

The flavor of the chowder improves if it is made a day in advance. Chill in the refrigerator until required, then reheat slowly to prevent the fish from disintegrating.

Clam and Pasta Soup

Subtly sweet and spicy, this soup is an ideal starter for a celebration dinner.

INGREDIENTS

Serves 4 to 6

2 tablespoons olive oil

1 onion, minced

leaves from 1 fresh or dried sprig of
   thyme, chopped or crumbled

2 garlic cloves, crushed

5 or 6 fresh basil leaves, plus extra
   to garnish

¼ to ½ teaspoon crushed red chilies,
   to taste

1 quart fish stock

1½ cups passata (strained, puréed
   tomatoes)

1 teaspoon granulated sugar

scant 1 cup frozen peas

⅔ cup small pasta shapes, such as
   chifferini

8 ounces frozen shelled clams

salt and freshly ground black pepper

1 Heat the oil in a large
   saucepan. Add the onion and
cook for about 5 minutes until soft
but not colored. Stir in the thyme,
garlic, basil leaves, and chilies.

2 Add the stock, passata, and
   sugar to the saucepan with salt
and pepper to taste and bring to a
boil. Lower the heat and simmer
for 15 minutes, stirring from time
to time. Add the frozen peas and
cook for 5 minutes longer.

3 Add the pasta to the stock
   mixture and bring to a boil,
stirring. Lower the heat and
simmer for about 5 minutes, or
according to the package directions,
stirring frequently, until the pasta
is *al dente*.

4 Turn the heat down to low,
   add the frozen clams, and heat
through for 2 to 3 minutes. Taste
and adjust the seasoning. Serve
hot in warm bowls, garnished with
basil leaves.

COOK'S TIP

Frozen shelled clams are
available at good fishmongers
and supermarkets. If you can't
get them, use bottled or canned
clams in natural juice (not
vinegar). Italian delicatessens sell
jars of clams in their shells.
These both look and taste
delicious and are not too
expensive. For a special occasion,
stir some into the soup.

Pasta Soup with Chicken Livers

A soup that can be served as a first or main course. The fried chicken livers are so delicious that, even if you do not normally like them, you may find yourself lapping them up in this soup.

INGREDIENTS

Serves 4 to 6

$\frac{1}{2}$ cup chicken livers, thawed
    if frozen

1 tablespoon olive oil

a pat of butter

4 garlic cloves, crushed

3 sprigs each of fresh parsley, marjoram,
    and sage, chopped

1 sprig of fresh thyme, chopped

5 or 6 fresh basil leaves, chopped

1–2 tablespoons dry white wine

2 x 11-ounce cans condensed chicken
    consommé

2 cups frozen peas

$\frac{1}{2}$ cup small pasta shapes, such as *farfalle*

2 or 3 scallions, sliced diagonally

salt and freshly ground black pepper

1 Cut the chicken livers into small pieces with scissors. Heat the oil and butter in a skillet. Add the garlic and herbs, with salt and ground black pepper to taste, and fry slowly for a few minutes. Add the livers, increase the heat to high, and stir-fry for a few minutes until they change color and become dry. Add the wine and cook until it evaporates. Remove from the heat.

2 Tip both cans of chicken consommé into a large saucepan and add water to the condensed soup as directed on the labels. Add an extra can of water, stir in a little salt and pepper, and bring to a boil.

3 Add the frozen peas to the pan and simmer for about 5 minutes. Add the small pasta shapes and return the soup to a boil, stirring. Leave to simmer, stirring frequently, for about 5 minutes, or according to the directions on the package, until the pasta is *al dente*.

4 Add the fried chicken livers and scallions and heat through for 2 to 3 minutes. Taste and adjust the seasoning. Serve hot, in warm bowls.

Ginger, Chicken, and Coconut Soup

This aromatic soup is rich with coconut milk and intensely flavored with galangal, lemongrass, and kaffir lime leaves.

INGREDIENTS

Serves 4 to 6

3 cups coconut milk

2 cups chicken stock

4 lemongrass stalks, bruised and chopped

1-inch piece ginger root, finely sliced

10 black peppercorns, crushed

10 kaffir lime leaves, torn

2½ cups skinless, boneless chicken cut
    into thin strips

1½ cups white mushrooms

½ cup baby corn cobs

4 tablespoons lime juice

3 tablespoons fish sauce

For the garnish

2 red chilies, chopped

3 or 4 scallions, chopped

chopped fresh cilantro

1 Bring the coconut milk and chicken stock to a boil in a saucepan. Add the lemongrass, ginger, peppercorns, and half the kaffir lime leaves. Lower the heat and simmer for 10 minutes.

2 Strain the stock into a clean pan. Return to the heat, add the chicken, white mushrooms, and baby corn. Simmer for 5 to 7 minutes until the chicken is cooked through.

3 Stir in the lime juice, fish sauce to taste, and the rest of the lime leaves. Serve hot, garnished with red chilies, scallions, and cilantro.

Indian Beef and Berry Soup

The fresh berries give this soup an unexpected kick.

INGREDIENTS

Serves 4

2 tablespoons vegetable oil

1 pound tender beef steak

2 onions, finely sliced

2 tablespoons butter

1 quart good beef stock or bouillon

½ teaspoon salt

1 cup fresh huckleberries, blueberries or blackberries, lightly mashed

1 tablespoon honey

1 Heat the oil in a heavy-bottomed saucepan until almost smoking. Add the steak and brown on both sides over medium-high heat. Remove the steak from the pan, set aside.

2 Lower the heat to low and add the sliced onions and butter to the pan. Stir well, scraping up the meat juices. Cook over low heat for 8 to 10 minutes until the onions are soft.

3 Add the beef stock or bouillon and salt and bring to a boil, stirring well. Stir in the mashed berries and the honey and simmer for 20 minutes.

4 Meanwhile, cut the steak into thin, bite-size slivers. Taste the soup and add more salt or honey if necessary. Add the steak to the pan. Simmer for 30 seconds, stirring all the time. Serve.

Index